Monte Carlo Simulation

The Art of Random Process Characterization

D. James Benton

Copyright © 2018 by D. James Benton, all rights reserved.

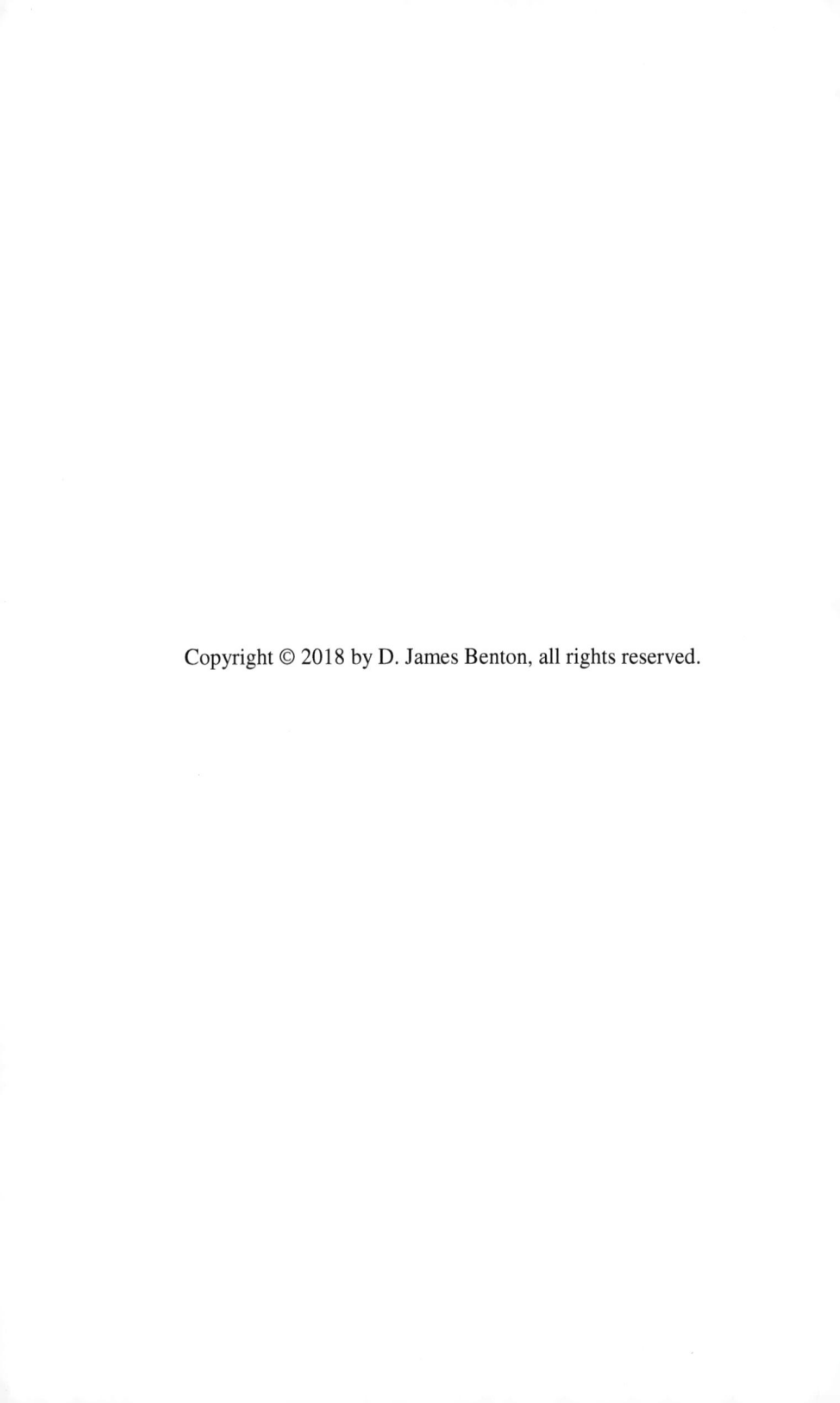

Foreword

There are many textbooks devoted to the theory behind Monte Carlo methods. More often than not, these are heavy on theory and light on example. Rarely do they include the examples in their entirety, mostly presenting the final results in summary form. The aim of this text is to be light on theory and heavy on example. Each example is included in its entirety: input, output, and source code or spreadsheet. If you work through all the examples, you should be able to simulate whatever process is needed.

All of the examples contained in this book,
(as well as a lot of free programs) are available at...
http://www.dudleybenton.altervista.org/software/index.html

Programming

Most of the examples in this book are implemented in Excel®. It's good enough for small things, but is quickly overwhelmed by large tasks. The truth is that Excel® is slower than a herd of snails stampeding up the side of a salt dome. So is MatLab®, Java®, and Python®. If you care about speed and efficiency, you should learn C. There's never been anything like it in the world of programming and I'm old enough to have seen them all. Check out Appendix H for an example of the amazing speed that can be achieved with raw executable code.

European
Single 0

American
Single and Double 0

Table of Contents

	page
Foreword	i
Programming	i
Chapter 1. Introduction	1
Chapter 2. Simple Threshold Examples	5
Chapter 3. Gambling Machines	11
Chapter 4. Normally-Distributed Parameters	16
Chapter 5. Log Normally-Distributed Parameters	22
Chapter 6. Shuffling	24
Chapter 7. Sampling	28
Chapter 8. Systematic Bias	34
Chapter 9. Traffic	37
Chapter 10. Solar Collectors	42
Chapter 11. Random Walk	47
Chapter 12. Weather	51
Chapter 13. Guessing	55
Appendix A: Random Number Generation	68
Appendix B. Two-Way & Three-Way Gunfight	73
Appendix C. Slot Machine Code	77
Appendix D. Slot Machine Code	79
Appendix E. Card Deck Shuffling Program	82
Appendix F. Systematic Bias Program	85
Appendix G. Diffusion Simulation Program	90
Appendix H. Password Synonym Finder	94

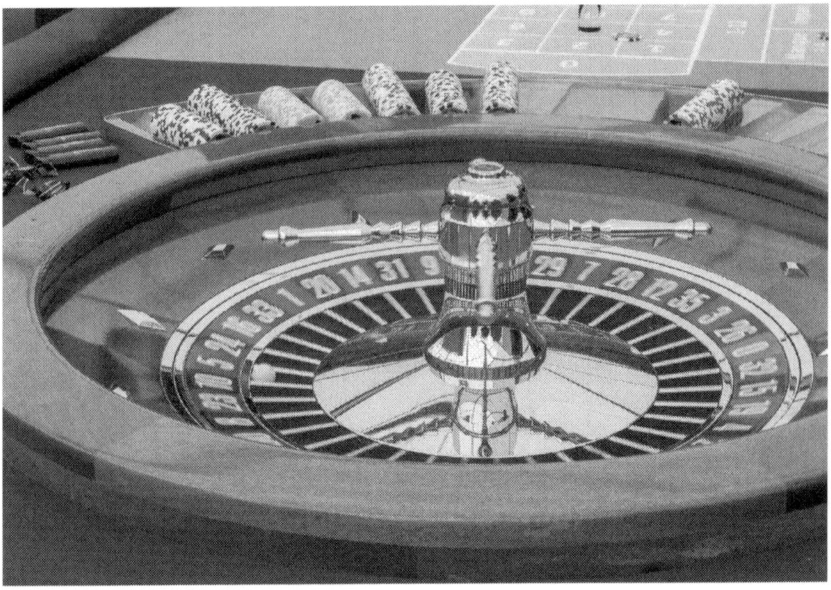

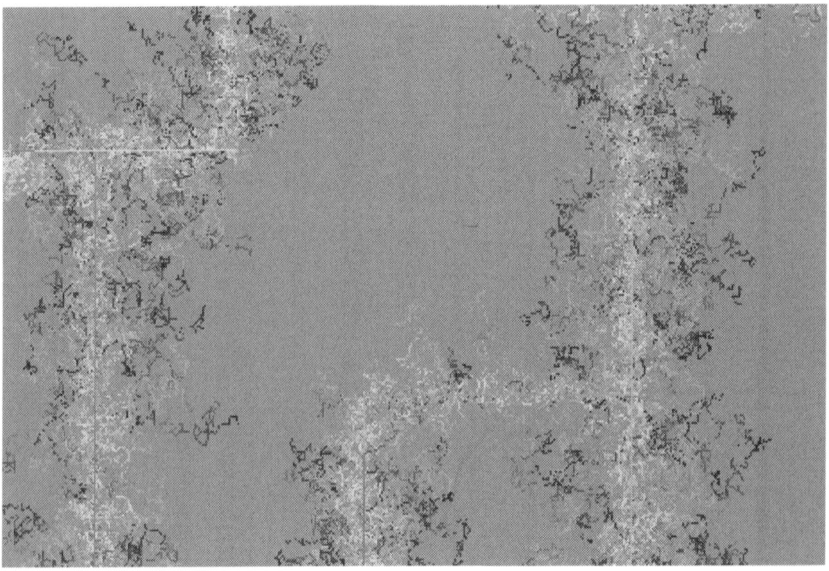

Chapter 1. Introduction

Scientists working on the atomic bomb in the 1940s applied this approach to problems that were too complicated to solve analytically and beyond the capability of available computers. They hoped to infer the behavior of complex systems by randomly sampling some of the possible outcomes, much like a gambler getting the feel of roulette by watching the wheel for a while and then placing a bet. This gaming analogy gave rise to the name *Monte Carlo*, after what was then the world's most famous casino.

This approach has been extended to include systems where we are uncertain of the exact inputs and/or the exact response. We may know a range of inputs or parameters as well as a range of responses. It is most often presumed that these vary around some mean, having some width or standard deviation.

Two types of parameters are considered: continuous and discrete. Parameters of the former type take on an infinite number of values over some range, while those of the latter take on only a finite number of discrete values. An example of the former would be: 0.145, 0.238, 0.485, etc. An example of the latter would be: 0 (off) or 1 (on).

Two types of variation are considered: random and systematic. The former are easily generated, whereas the latter are not. In reality, very few things are truly random. It can even be argued that nothing is truly random—including random numbers. Some phenomena clearly exhibit systematic (i.e., non-random) behavior. We will consider in some detail how these may be characterized for the purpose of simulation.

Two types of parameters are considered: independent and dependent or uncorrelated and correlated. The former can take on a range of values without consideration of any other, whereas the latter are in some way limited by one or more of the others. We will consider both types—how they occur and how to generate them for use in a simulation.

Random Integers

Two types of random integers will be considered: uniformly-distributed and normally-distributed. These are illustrated in the following figure. Uniformly-distributed random numbers are equally likely, whereas normally-distributed random numbers cluster symmetrically around a single value such that their frequency of occurrence forms a bell-shaped curve.

The C function rand() returns uniformly-distributed integers between 0 and 32767 (that is, positive 15-bit values). The Excel® function rand() and VBA® function Rnd() return uniformly-distributed real values between 0 and 1, which are actually 15-bit positive integers divided by 32767. More details are provided in Appendix A, including how these may be used to create larger integers and normally-distributed random numbers. The following figure and calculations may be found in the spreadsheet random_numbers.xls in the on-line archive.

The algorithm in this spreadsheet doesn't work quite right (not enough of the larger integers) which gives rise to the downward tail on the right side of the blue line. In spite of this, it's still adequate for our purposes.

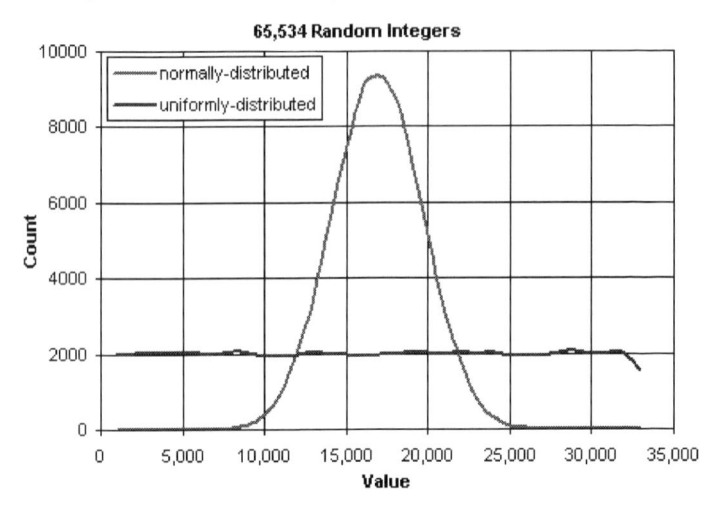

65,534 Random Integers

Random Floating-Point Numbers

There are two principal categories of random floating-point (i.e., real) numbers: linear and logarithmic. In the case of normally-distributed, values of the former exhibit a bell-shaped curve, whereas the logs of the latter exhibit this familiar shape. There are more types of real numbers than integers, including: harmonic (which might arise from vibrations or sound), radial, cylindrical, spherical, etc. We will also consider some of these.

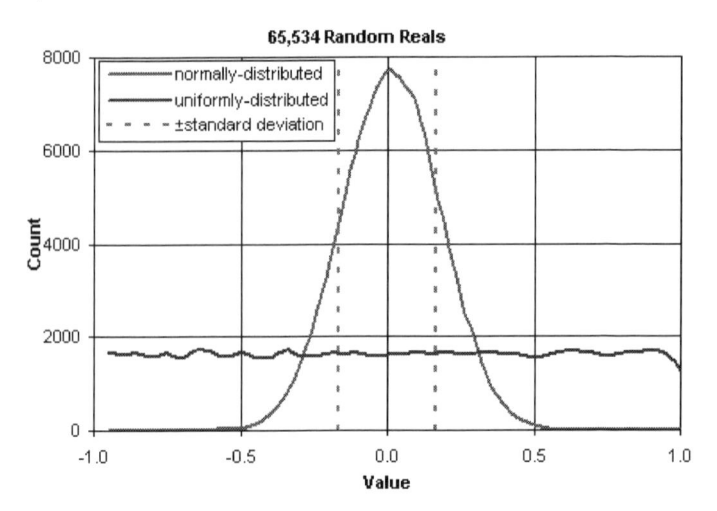

65,534 Random Reals

Not surprisingly, these two graphs are quite similar. After all, the random reals are generated from the random integers. These have a mean (average) of zero and a standard deviation of 1/6th. The bell-shaped red curve is the normal distribution. The probability density (i.e., the bell-shaped curve) is given by the following formula:

$$f(\mu,\sigma,x) = \frac{1}{\sqrt{2\pi\sigma^2}} e^{\left[\frac{(x-\mu)^2}{2\sigma^2}\right]} \qquad (1.1)$$

$$p(\mu,\sigma,x) = \int_{-\infty}^{x} f(\mu,\sigma,x)dx \qquad (1.2)$$

The probability (i.e., the area under the bell-shaped curve) doesn't have a closed-form solution, but can be readily calculated using the Excel® function NORMDIST(). Both are illustrated in the following figure:

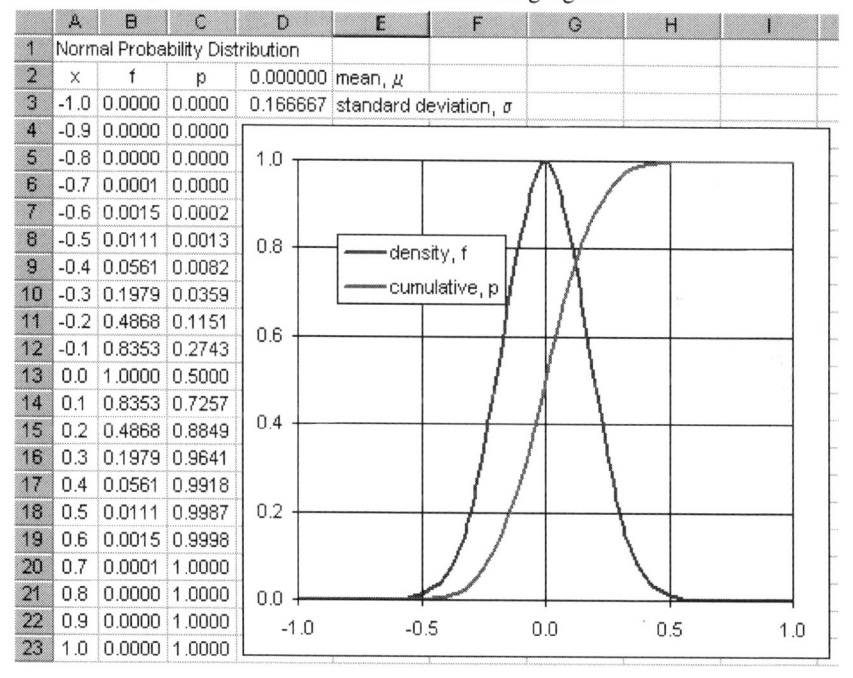

	A	B	C	D	E	F	G	H	I
1	Normal Probability Distribution								
2	x	f	p	0.000000	mean, μ				
3	-1.0	0.0000	0.0000	0.166667	standard deviation, σ				
4	-0.9	0.0000	0.0000						
5	-0.8	0.0000	0.0000						
6	-0.7	0.0001	0.0000						
7	-0.6	0.0015	0.0002						
8	-0.5	0.0111	0.0013						
9	-0.4	0.0561	0.0082						
10	-0.3	0.1979	0.0359						
11	-0.2	0.4868	0.1151						
12	-0.1	0.8353	0.2743						
13	0.0	1.0000	0.5000						
14	0.1	0.8353	0.7257						
15	0.2	0.4868	0.8849						
16	0.3	0.1979	0.9641						
17	0.4	0.0561	0.9918						
18	0.5	0.0111	0.9987						
19	0.6	0.0015	0.9998						
20	0.7	0.0001	1.0000						
21	0.8	0.0000	1.0000						
22	0.9	0.0000	1.0000						
23	1.0	0.0000	1.0000						

The 68-95-99.7 Rule

It is often assumed that test scores and population measures such as IQ, size, weight, etc. are normally-distributed. This gives rise to the 68-95-99.7 rule, which is: 68% of the population fall within $-\sigma$ to $+\sigma$, that is, they lie within ± one standard deviation of the mean. Ninety-five percent of the population lie within ±2σ and 99.7% lie within ±3σ. These boundaries arise from Equation 1.2: p(±σ), p(±2σ), and p(±3σ). Graphically, this means that about 68% of the total area under the blue curve lies between -σ and +σ, etc.

This background on random numbers is preparation for the Monte Carlo simulations to follow. Basically, generating random numbers is the equivalent of tossing dice, spinning a wheel, or drawing a card. We must understand how the random numbers are generated in order to assure that they produce the right behavior to mimic the dice, wheel, or cards, otherwise our simulations will not accurately represent the processes we hope to characterize by our sampling.

Chapter 2. Simple Threshold Examples

In this chapter we will consider four very simple examples: coin toss, quick draw (two-way and three-way), and battling monsters. These are arranged in order of increasing complexity. The coin toss has only one decision point or branch. The second considers both speed and accuracy so that it has two decision points plus a third gunslinger. The fourth has a more complicated decision than merely heads or tails. These are all based on comparing thresholds.

Gambler's Ruin

This is the simplest example of a gambling simulation. There are two players (Andy and Bart). Each starts with a certain amount of money. They toss a coin. If it comes up heads, Andy wins $1. If it comes up tails, Bart wins $1. The game continues until one player is broke. This is easily implemented in an Excel® spreadsheet. All we need is a way to randomly determine heads or tails. This is equivalent to odd or even, which in C is i%2 and in VB is i MOD 2. The code is very simple:

```
Function irand() As Integer
  irand = Rnd() * 32767#
End Function
Function winner(ByVal Acash As Integer, ByVal Bcash As
    Integer) As Variant
  Dim toss As Integer
  toss = 0
  While (True)
    toss = toss + 1
    If (irand() Mod 2) Then
      Acash = Acash + 1
      Bcash = Bcash - 1
      If (Bcash <= 0) Then
        winner = Array("Andy", toss)
        Exit Function
      End If
    Else
      Acash = Acash - 1
      Bcash = Bcash + 1
      If (Acash <= 0) Then
        winner = Array("Bart", toss)
        Exit Function
      End If
    End If
  Wend
End Function
```

The qualifier ByVal in function winner() is necessary to keep a variable passed into this function (which is done inside the simulation loop) from changing in value during execution of the function. The result are shown in this next figure:

	A	B	C	D	E	F	G	H	I	J	K
1	Gambler's Ruin			Andy	Bart						
2	game	winner	toss	$5	$7	push to run simulation					
3	1	Andy	33								
4	2	Bart	7			65,536 Simulated Games					
5	3	Andy	31			starting cash		ning percent		tosses	
6	4	Andy	17			Andy	Bart	Andy	Bart	avg	max
7	5	Bart	67			$3	$3	50%	50%	9	79
8	6	Bart	57			$3	$5	37%	63%	15	173
9	7	Bart	67			$3	$7	30%	70%	22	231
10	8	Andy	9			$3	$9	25%	75%	28	359
11	9	Bart	17			$5	$3	63%	37%	15	157
12	10	Bart	17			$5	$5	50%	50%	26	235
13	11	Bart	19			$5	$7	41%	59%	36	297
14	12	Bart	17			$5	$9	36%	64%	46	485
15	13	Bart	81			$7	$3	70%	30%	21	263
16	14	Bart	9			$7	$5	58%	42%	36	301
17	15	Bart	31			$7	$7	50%	50%	50	485
18	16	Bart	59			$7	$9	44%	56%	64	541
19	17	Bart	5			$9	$3	75%	25%	28	337
20	18	Andy	21			$9	$5	64%	36%	46	447
21	19	Bart	25			$9	$7	56%	44%	64	477
22	20	Bart	11			$9	$9	50%	50%	83	853

Not surprisingly, the gambler with the most money to start with almost always wins (i.e., the *house*). The number of coin tosses before ruin increases with the amount of initial cash, perhaps increasing the false impression that the mark won't lose his paycheck again this week. This game and so many others like it are rather foolish.

The Gunfight

The second example we will consider is a classic gunfight—every movie about the Wild West must have at least one. Andy and Bart step into the dusty street outside the saloon and square off for a duel. We will consider two aspects of these gunslingers: accuracy and speed. Neither is perfectly consistent in his performance, which may depend on many things, including how much liquor was consumed in the saloon before the challenge.

Our simulation is a series of tests (if...then statements). If Andy fires first, then... or if Bart fires first, then... If the one firing first delivers a fatal shot, the duel is over, otherwise the slower draw fires a shot. This second bullet may or may not be fatal. This process continues until one is dead. This simulation is easily implemented in an Excel® spreadsheet (gunfight.xls in downloadable the on-line archive).

	A	B	C	D	E	F
1	quick draw			A	B	gunman
2	duel	winner	shots	50%	75%	accuracy
3	1	2	1	75%	50%	speed
4	2	1	1	43.1%	56.9%	winner
5	3	2	1	shots	count	percent
6	4	1	1	1	877	88%
7	5	2	1	2	103	10%
8	6	2	1	3	18	2%
9	7	1	1	4	2	0%
10	8	1	1	5	0	0%
11	9	1	1		1000	
12	10	1	1			
13	11	2	1			
14	12	2	1			
15	13	2	1			
16	14	2	1			
17	15	2	1			
18	16	2	1			
19	17	1	2			

Andy has been assigned a fatal-shot accuracy of 50% and Bart 75%. Andy has been assigned a quick draw speed better than 75% of his peers, while Bart's draw is average at 50%. Andy prevails 43.1% of the time compared to Bart at 56.9%, which goes against the old adage: *shoot first and hope you don't miss*. According to this simulation, accuracy is more important than speed.

You can change the percentages and see what happens to the outcome. The spreadsheet will update automatically. In this case 88% of the duels end after the fist shot and 98% after the second. Only 20 times out of 1000 were 3 or more shots fired. The logic (or code) that serves as a model for this process is:

```
Function duel(Aacc As Double, Aspd As Double, Bacc As
    Double, Bspd As Double) As Variant
  Dim shot As Integer
  shot = 0
  While (True)
    shot = shot + 1
    If (Aspd * Rnd() > Bspd * Rnd()) Then
      If (Aacc >= Rnd()) Then
        duel = Array(1, shot)
        Exit Function
      ElseIf (Bacc >= Rnd()) Then
        duel = Array(2, shot)
        Exit Function
      End If
    Else
      If (Bacc >= Rnd()) Then
        duel = Array(2, shot)
        Exit Function
      ElseIf (Aacc >= Rnd()) Then
        duel = Array(1, shot)
        Exit Function
      End If
```

7

```
End If
Wend
End Function
```

The Rnd() function is used to provide uniform random real numbers between 0 and 1, which is what we want for this process. We have no target mean or standard deviation representing a normally distributed expectation of outcomes. This sequence of calculations is adequate, appropriate, and produces reasonable results.

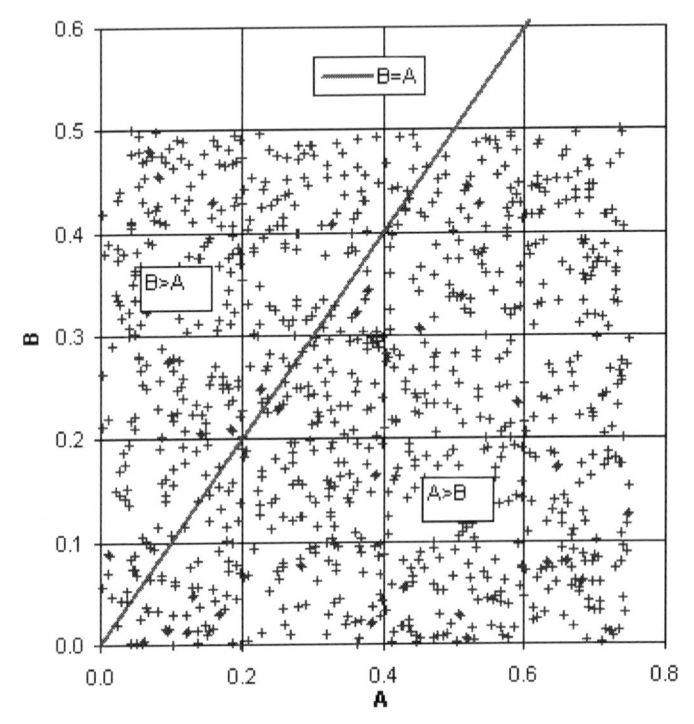

In this case, the random number generated is compared to a *threshold*. If the threshold is met or exceeded the associated result occurs, otherwise it does not. This is the simplest type of simulation. A test of this type can be illustrated in the preceding figure, where A is the simulated speed of Andy (75%) and B is the simulated speed of Bart (50%). The blue +s below the red line (B=A) satisfy A>B, thus Andy prevails. The blue +s above the red line satisfy B>A, thus Bart prevails. As expected, about 75% of the blue +s are below the red line and 25% are above.

Three-Way Gunfight

The most famous 3-way gunfight is a scene from the 1966 movie *The Good, The Bad, and The Ugly* starring Clint Eastwood (as Blondie), Lee Van Cleef (as

Angel Eyes), and Eli Wallach (as Tuco). Not only is there an additional contestant, each must decide how he compares to the other two and they to each other. There are many ways this can play out. The most lethal of the three is likely to first shoot the second most lethal—presuming he right about this ranking in this case. The second is most likely to first shoot the most lethal. The third is most likely to shoot the first, hoping the first will kill the second.

We will model this 3-way contest by adding a confidence factor to each. This confidence factor indicates the certainty of each gunman in picking the most lethal of the other two. Again, we are considering thresholds and will only require uniformly-distributed random numbers. The nest of if…then statements needed to properly handle this in Excel® would be quite large indeed. Instead, we will use C, which is much more versatile. Rather than creating an entire nest of if…then statements for each case A>B&C, B>A&C, C>A&B, we will use an array of structures representing the 3 gunslingers and sort them fast to slow.

This contains the logic for both two-way and three-way duels, as the latter reduces to the former after one of the gunslingers is dead. In each round we consider which fires first, if his shot is lethal, and whom he shot. If the first to draw picked the right one and his shot was lethal, then the second to draw dies, otherwise the third to draw dies. If the second to draw survives (i.e., the first either missed or shot the third) we must consider if his shot was lethal and whom he shot. If the third to draw is still alive (i.e., the first two either missed or shot each other) we consider whether he was lucky enough to shoot the other live gunslinger. This process continues until only one is left. The code is listed in Appendix B.

```
Blondie    vs. AngelEyes survivor: Blondie    after 2 shots
Blondie    vs. AngelEyes survivor: Blondie    after 1 shot
Blondie    vs. AngelEyes survivor: Blondie    after 1 shot
Blondie    vs. AngelEyes survivor: Blondie    after 2 shots
Blondie    vs. AngelEyes survivor: Blondie    after 1 shot
Blondie    vs. Tuco      survivor: Blondie    after 1 shot
Blondie    vs. Tuco      survivor: Blondie    after 1 shot
Blondie    vs. Tuco      survivor: Blondie    after 1 shot
Blondie    vs. Tuco      survivor: Tuco       after 2 shots
Blondie    vs. Tuco      survivor: Blondie    after 2 shots
AngelEyes  vs. Tuco      survivor: Tuco       after 2 shots
AngelEyes  vs. Tuco      survivor: Tuco       after 2 shots
AngelEyes  vs. Tuco      survivor: Tuco       after 1 shot
AngelEyes  vs. Tuco      survivor: Tuco       after 1 shot
AngelEyes  vs. Tuco      survivor: Tuco       after 1 shot
Blondie vs. AngelEyes vs. Tuco survivor: AngelEyes after 1 shot
Blondie vs. AngelEyes vs. Tuco survivor: Tuco      after 2 shots
Blondie vs. AngelEyes vs. Tuco survivor: Tuco      after 2 shots
Blondie vs. AngelEyes vs. Tuco survivor: Blondie   after 3 shots
Blondie vs. AngelEyes vs. Tuco survivor: AngelEyes after 2 shots
```

Battling Monsters

The final example is a little more complicated. We will consider battles between three types of monsters: an orc (challenge rating 4) and a troll (challenge rating 5) and a hydra (challenge rating 8). We want the battle performance of these monsters to be positive, on average equal to their challenge rating, and normally-distributed (that is, exhibit a bell-shaped curve). This is easily accomplished by multiplying their challenge rating by a normally-distributed random real number ranging from 0 to 1.

The random number is easily generated by averaging a dozen uniformly-distributed random numbers supplied by the Excel® function Rnd(), as described in Appendix A. The performance during each battle is calculated by multiplying by the respective challenge rating. All of the calculations can be readily implemented in a spreadsheet (monster.xls).

In order to produce smooth curves, at least 10,000 samples are required. This takes quite a while for Excel® to update because the statistics are recalculated each time the random numbers are updated in a vicious cycle. In order to avoid this inefficient process, a button has been provided in the spreadsheet that updates 65,534 samples in a few seconds. The results are shown in the following figure:

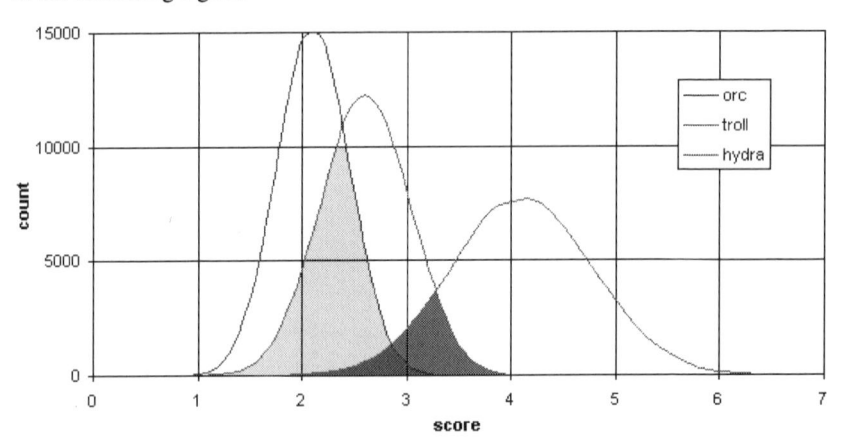

The area under all three curves is the same: 65,534 (i.e., the number of battles). The orc scores lower more often (i.e., the blue curve is to the left and taller). The hydra scores higher less often (i.e., the red curve is to the right and shorter). The troll scores between these two. The overlapping regions have been shaded. The magenta plus green regions are battles where the troll defeats the hydra. The yellow plus green regions are where the orc defeats the troll. The green region is where the orc defeats the hydra.

Chapter 3. Gambling Machines

Some examples of gambling machines are: roulette wheels and slots. The same principles apply lottery tickets and scratch-off coupons. In these cases, Monte Carlo simulations aren't necessary, because the *odds* can be calculated algebraically. These are still useful examples and provide an opportunity to test the simulation because the solution is known.

Roulette

Consider the following spreadsheet (roulette.xls) for our first example:

	A	B	C	D	E	F	G	H	I	J	K	L	M	N	O	P
1					1	2	3	4	6	12	18	18	odds*38		wheel	
2					35	17	11	8	5	2	1	1	payout	pos	val	clr
3					94.7%	94.7%	94.7%	94.7%	94.7%	94.7%	94.7%	94.7%	player	1	0	G
4					5.3%	5.3%	5.3%	5.3%	5.3%	5.3%	5.3%	5.3%	house	2	28	B
5					94.7%	95.2%	94.6%	97.3%	97.3%	95.5%	94.0%	93.6%	simulation	3	9	R
6	spin	pos	val	clr	1	1,2	1,2,3	1,2,4,5	1-6	1-12	R	odd	bet	4	26	B
7	1	28	31	B	0	0	0	0	0	0	0	2		5	30	R
8	2	22	10	B	0	0	0	0	0	3	0	0		6	11	B
9	3	37	14	R	0	0	0	0	0	0	2	0		7	7	R
10	4	31	21	R	0	0	0	0	0	0	2	2		8	20	B
11	5	14	15	B	0	0	0	0	0	0	0	2		9	32	R
12	6	2	28	B	0	0	0	0	0	0	0	0		10	17	B
13	7	15	3	R	0	0	12	0	6	3	2	2		11	5	R
14	8	38	2	B	0	18	12	9	6	3	0	0		12	22	B

Row six columns E through L contain eight types of bets: a single number (in this case 1), two numbers (1,2), three numbers (1,2,3), four numbers (1,2,4,5), six numbers (1-6), twelve numbers (1-12), a color (red), and odd or even (in this case odd). Row 1 contains the odds for each bet times 38, that is: 1 out of 38 (denoted 1:38), 2 out of 38 (2:38), and so forth up to 18 out of 38. The payout is in row 2 (i.e., what's added to your chips if you win).

The *return* on this game or the long-term rate of recovery (if you had all the time and money in the world to waste) for each bet is equal to (payout+1)*odds or (row2+1)*(row1/38). The result appears in row 3 and is 94.7% for all bets. The difference in every case is 5.3%, which is called the *house advantage*. This is what the owner of the wheel can expect to keep in the long run. The house doesn't care how much money you win because they're going to get it back eventually.

This spreadsheet contains 10,000 spins (i.e., the sample size of our Monte Carlo Simulation is 10,000). The results appear in cells A7:D10006: the spin, the position on the wheel (see cells N3:P40), the value (match column B to column N and return column O), and the color (match column B to column N and return column P). There are if…then statements in cells E7:L10006 that compare each spin (columns A through D) to each bet (row 6 columns E through L), listing the payout (row 2) for each win.

Row 5 contains the sum of each column divided by the number of columns and is the calculated *return* for the simulation. Row 5 columns E through L are reasonably close to row 3, indicating that the simulation is a success in that it is tending toward the known analytical solution. Our technique is working.

Slots

Some believe in the Force and others in Luck. The former are drawn to galactic wars and the latter to gambling. There's one thing you can be sure of in a game of chance: the house always wins in the end. The opulent casino and racetrack should be all the proof of this you need. Slot machines are perhaps the worst form of gambling as far as the rate of return is concerned. This is what a slot machine *one-armed bandit* looks like on the inside:

What you may not know is that the wheels aren't the same. That is, they don't have the same pictures on them. The wheels are designed to give you the impression of having a greater chance of winning than you actually do. This visual trickery provides an additional advantage for the house, much like the ordering of numbers and colors on the roulette wheel is designed to confuse the player. These tables show how the pictures work into odds.

There are 3 bars on the first reel, but only 2 on the second and 1 on the third. There are 21 pictures total on each reel. Rather than your chances of getting 3 bars in a row being $(3/21)^3 = 1/343$, they're only $(3/21)*(2/21)*(1/21) = 2/3087$. A payback of 1000:1 for odds of 1:343 sounds too good to be true because it is. The odds are actually 1:1544 and the return is only $1000*(2/3087)$ or 64.8%. The house keeps 35.2% in the long run, making slots a far more foolish game than roulette. In fact, slots are 6.7 times as lucrative for the house than roulette plus they don't have to pay a spinner.

	A	B	C	D	E	F	G	H
1		Slot Machine or "One-Armed-Bandit"						
2	reel 1	reel 2	reel 3		picture	reel 1	reel 2	reel 3
3	bar	bar	bar		bar	3	2	1
4	cherry	plum	orange		cherry	3	3	2
5	orange	bell	lemon		plum	3	4	3
6	bell	orange	bell		bell	4	4	4
7	plum	lemon	plum		orange	4	4	5
8	bar	bar	orange		lemon	4	4	6
9	cherry	cherry	cherry		total	21	21	21
10	lemon	plum	bell					
11	bell	bell	lemon					
12	plum	orange	orange					
13	orange	lemon	plum					
14	lemon	cherry	lemon					
15	bell	plum	cherry					
16	plum	bell	orange					
17	orange	orange	lemon					
18	cherry	lemon	bell					
19	lemon	plum	orange					
20	bar	bell	lemon					
21	orange	orange	bell					
22	bell	lemon	plum					
23	lemon	cherry	lemon					

The odds, payout, and rate of return are shown in this next figure:

J	K	L	M	N	O	P
	payout, chance, probaility, and rate of return					
spin	pay	chance	prob	Σprob	return	Σreturn
3 bars	170	6:9261	0.00065	0.00065	11.0%	11.0%
3 cherries	56	18:9261	0.00194	0.00259	10.9%	21.9%
3 plums	28	36:9261	0.00389	0.00648	10.9%	32.8%
3 bells	16	64:9261	0.00691	0.01339	11.1%	43.8%
3 oranges	12	80:9261	0.00864	0.02203	10.4%	54.2%
3 lemons	10	96:9261	0.01037	0.03239	10.4%	64.6%
2 bars	4	231:9261	0.02494	0.05734	10.0%	74.5%
2 cherries	2	441:9261	0.04762	0.10496	9.5%	84.1%
2 plums	1	693:9261	0.07483	**0.17979**	7.5%	**91.6%**
2 bells	1	1008:9261	0.10884	0.28863	10.9%	102.4%
2 oranges	1	1176:9261	0.12698	0.41561	12.7%	115.1%
2 lemons	1	1344:9261	0.14512	0.56074	14.5%	129.7%

On row 3 we see that three bars pays out 170 coins and has a chance of 6 out of 9261 or a probability of 0.00065. The 6 comes from the number of bars on each of the three reels (3*2*1=6) and the 9261 comes from the total number of pictures on each reel (21^3=9261). The return for this particular combination is the probability times the payout or 11% (column O). The probabilities are accumulated in column N and the returns are accumulated in column P. At 2 plums the accumulated probability reaches 0.17979, meaning the machine on average pays out something almost 18% of the time or once every 5 or 6 pulls, which is enough to keep gamblers from being too discouraged. The accumulated return at this point is 91.6%. Any farther down in the table (for example 2 bells) and the payout exceeds 100% (on average, the machine would lose money).

The payout must be adjusted so that some reward is given often enough to string people along, but not too often so that the owner of the machine makes money. The return for each combination (column O) is approximately the same, which gives the appearance of reasonable fairness and expectation. In the case of coin operated machines, the payout (column K) must be an integer. These factors must be balanced with the pictures on the reels in order to make this seem less foolish while emptying your pockets. This machine is very easy to simulate, as illustrated in the spreadsheet and below:

R	S	T	U	V	W	X
		Monte Carlo Simulation				
pull	reel 1	reel 2	reel 3	payout	sum	return
1	lemon	orange	cherry	0	0	0%
2	lemon	bell	lemon	0	0	0%
3	plum	cherry	bell	0	0	0%
4	cherry	bar	bar	4	4	100%
5	cherry	bar	bar	4	8	160%
6	lemon	orange	orange	0	8	133%
7	bell	orange	cherry	0	8	114%
8	plum	orange	bar	0	8	100%
9	bell	bell	orange	0	8	89%
10	bar	bell	plum	0	8	80%
90	bell	bell	lemon	0	58	64%
91	bar	cherry	bell	0	58	64%
92	cherry	orange	lemon	0	58	63%
93	cherry	bell	plum	0	58	62%
94	plum	cherry	bell	0	58	62%
95	plum	bar	orange	0	58	61%
96	lemon	plum	orange	0	58	60%
97	bar	plum	bell	0	58	60%
98	plum	plum	plum	28	86	88%
99	bar	orange	bell	0	86	87%
100	orange	plum	plum	1	87	87%

The spreadsheet simulation has 100 pulls. You can update it by pressing F9. You will often see the return go above 100% early on, but it will eventually fall off to 91.6% if you pull the lever enough times. This is the lure of the slot machine: sometimes you can win big. If you won big the first time, then quit and

14

never put in another coin, you'd be better off, but this isn't how people behave. The occasional gambler who wins big is drawn back again and again to lose all that and more. Ultimately, the house always wins in the long run. The calculations are quite simple. The code listed in Appendix C will suffice as a Monte Carlo Simulation set to run 1,000,000 pulls. The results are summarized in the following figure:

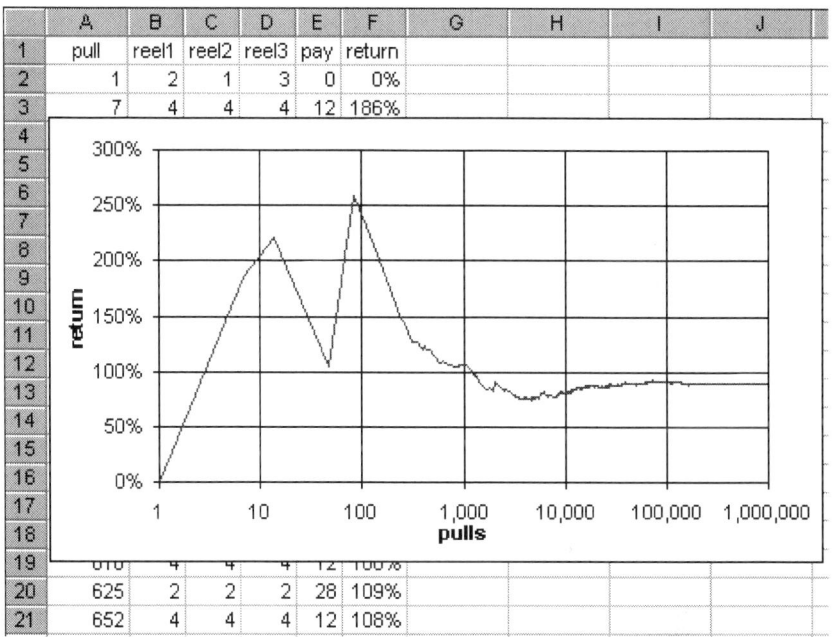

	A	B	C	D	E	F	G	H	I	J
1	pull	reel1	reel2	reel3	pay	return				
2	1	2	1	3	0	0%				
3	7	4	4	4	12	186%				
...										
19	610	4	4	4	12	100%				
20	625	2	2	2	28	109%				
21	652	4	4	4	12	108%				

I intentionally picked a starting point that would give the appearance of large winnings early on (186% payout on the seventh pull), but in the end it levels out to 91.6%, leaving 8.4% for the owner of the machine, an even bigger cut for the house than the roulette wheel.

15

Chapter 4. Normally-Distributed Parameters

We will now consider problems involving parameters that vary over a range in a particular way: the values are normally-distributed. We introduced such numbers in Chapter 1. Normally distributed parameters are usually characterized by their mean and standard deviation. IQ, height, and weight are three commonly recognized parameters that fit this pattern, provided the sample size is large enough.

The following figure (IQs.xls) contains 65,536 IQ scores generated randomly as described in Chapter 1 and Appendix A. The blue symbols indicate the number of occurrences of each score and the red curve is the ideal distribution as provided by the Excel® function NORMDIST(). For this sample size (65,536 points) the agreement is quite good.

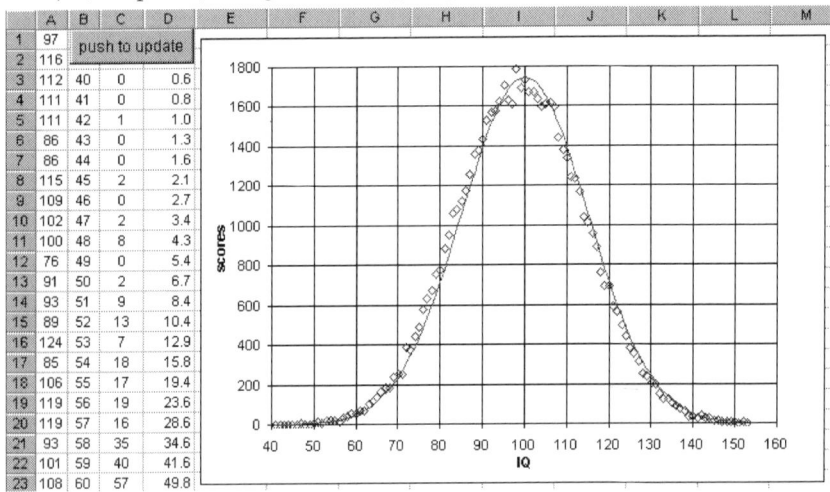

Bearing Clearance

For our first illustration we will consider a simple problem of clearance (i.e., the space between two machined objects), in this case a shaft and sleeve. The accuracy of the machines producing such parts is often characterized as normally-distributed random variations. This example is the greased sleeve bearing on a typical one horsepower electric motor. The shaft is nominally 5/8" (0.625 inch) in order for this bearing to work properly, the clearance must be 0.001250±0.000625 inch. The standard deviation of the machining process (boring for the sleeve and turning for the shaft) is 0.000200 inch.

We can easily set this problem up as an Excel® spreadsheet. The first ten rows contain the simulation parameters and labels. The simulation begins on row 11 and continues on to row 65,536. Column A contains the sleeve diameter, column B contains the shaft diameter, and column C contains the clearance. Column D contains a zero or one depending on whether the sleeve/shaft pair must be rejected (i.e., outside the allowable clearance range). There are 1695 rejects (cell D9) or 2.59% of the total, which is disappointing, but acceptable.

simulation parameters					0.62400	sleeve	shaft	0.00000	clearance
0.626250	0.625000	0.001250	target		0.62405	0	0	0.00005	1
0.000200	0.000200	0.000625	tolerance		0.62410	0	0	0.00010	0
simulation summary results				allowable	0.62415	0	0	0.00015	0
0.627039	0.625803	0.002340	max	0.001875	0.62420	0	0	0.00020	3
0.626249	0.625001	0.001248	avg	0.001250	0.62425	0	1	0.00025	6
0.625472	0.624246	-0.000011	min	0.000625	0.62430	0	11	0.00030	11
0.000199	0.000200	0.000282	stdev		0.62435	0	20	0.00035	28
simulation			1695	2.59%	0.62440	0	46	0.00040	38
sleeve	shaft	clearance	reject		0.62445	0	90	0.00045	63
0.626513	0.624751	0.001762	0		0.62450	0	169	0.00050	103

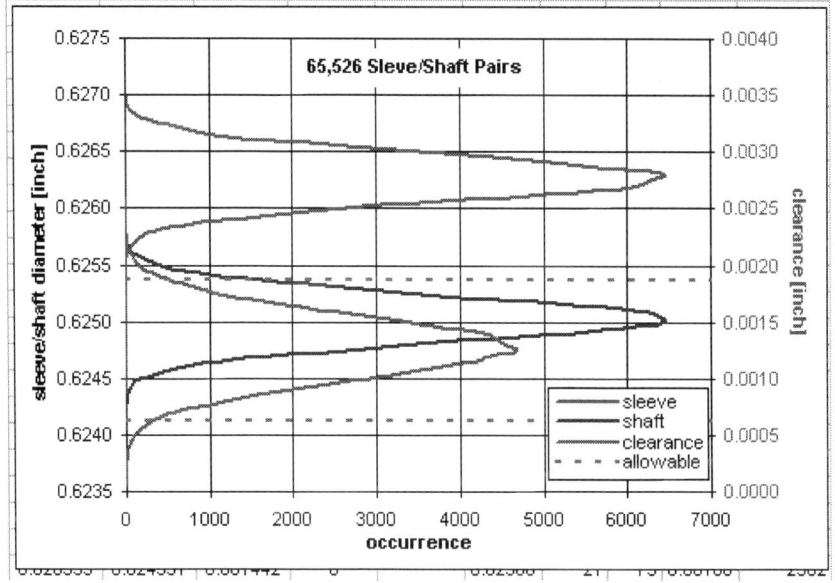

The maximum clearance is 0.002340 (cell C5), which is highlighted in red with conditional formatting because it's above the maximum (0.001875 cell E5). The minimum clearance is -0.000011 (cell C7) and is also highlighted in red because it's below the minimum (0.000625 cell E7). The sleeve diameter (green curve), shaft diameter (blue curve), and clearance (red curve) all exhibit the familiar bell shape. The sleeve and shaft diameters are inputs to the model and the clearance is simply the difference of the two, so this is not surprising.

This figure illustrates something you will see elsewhere in this book: a second Y-axis. The clearance is on a considerably different scale than the sleeve and shaft diameters and so must be plotted against a different axis. The sleeve and shaft diameter is plotted on the left Y-axis and the clearance is plotted on the right Y-axis. The label indicates this and so does the color of the numbers. I have intentionally made the numbers and text on the second (i.e., right) Y-axis

17

match the color of the curve that's plotted against that axis (i.e., the red one, clearance). The allowable limits on clearance are also shown (the dashed horizontal magenta lines).

Heat Exchanger

In the previous simulation (sleeve/shaft clearance), the output (clearance) was a simple combination of the inputs (sleeve and shaft diameters). The inputs were normally distributed and so was the output. In this next example we will consider a more complex relationship between inputs and outputs as well as more than two inputs.

A performance test was conducted on a large heat exchanger. The flows and temperatures (inlet and outlet) were measured, but these parameters cannot be determined precisely, as is often presumed. Instead, these values are only known to some level of certainty, as indicated in the spreadsheet heat_exchanger.xls and shown below:

	A	B	C	D	E	F	G	H	I
1	Monte Carlo Heat Exchanger Simulation (65,525 cases)								
2	name	units	mean	std.dev.					
3	mH	kg/s	4.00	0.40	push to update				
4	CpH	kJ/kg/°C	3.50	0.05					
5	mC	kg/s	9.00	0.90					
6	CpC	kJ/kg/°C	2.50	0.04					
7	THi	°C	500	0.67					
8	THo	°C	300	0.67					
9	TCi	°C	250	0.50					
10	TCo	°C	375	0.50					
11	case	mH	CpH	mC	CpC	THi	THo	TCi	TCo
12	1	3.769	3.470	8.948	2.547	500.0	299.4	249.9	375.5
13	2	3.853	3.510	10.047	2.466	500.0	299.7	250.1	374.4
14	3	3.465	3.518	8.547	2.405	500.0	300.4	249.9	375.2
15	4	3.977	3.547	9.853	2.500	499.3	299.4	250.6	374.6
16	5	3.497	3.510	7.342	2.500	499.7	298.4	250.2	374.9
17	6	4.453	3.521	8.481	2.500	499.8	300.1	249.3	375.2
18	7	3.993	3.575	7.757	2.500	500.1	299.9	250.4	375.0
19	8	4.067	3.467	8.658	2.500	500.0	300.9	249.3	375.2
20	9	4.227	3.512	9.272	2.500	500.0	301.0	249.6	374.9
21	10	4.421	3.505	8.586	2.500	499.9	299.6	249.5	375.8

Here, m_H and m_C are the hot and cold side flows, respectively. Cp_H and Cp_C are the hot and cold side constant pressure specific heats, respectively. T_{HI}, T_{HO}, T_{CI}, and T_{CO} are the hot and cold side inlet and outlet temperatures, respectively. The hot and cold side heat transfer (Q_H and Q_C) should be the same, but they are not and are calculated as follows:

$$Q_H = \dot{m}_H Cp_H \left(T_{H,out} - T_{H,in}\right) \quad (4.1)$$

$$Q_C = \dot{m}_C Cp_C \left(T_{C,in} - T_{C,out}\right) \quad (4.2)$$

These quantities are listed in the spreadsheet as illustrated below:

					QH			QC	
QH=	QC=		UAH=	UAC=	282	stdev		281	stdev	
mH*cpH	mC*cpC	LMTD	QH	QC	3909	max	analy-	3873	max	analy-
*(THi-	*(TCo-		/	/	2800	avg	tical	2813	avg	tical
THo)	TCi)		LMTD	LMTD	1681	min	model	1702	min	model
2623	2861	81.35	32.25	35.17	1726	0.00%	0.00%	1746	0.00%	0.00%
2709	3078	81.78	33.13	37.64	1770	0.00%	0.01%	1789	0.00%	0.01%
2434	2577	82.12	29.64	31.38	1815	0.01%	0.01%	1832	0.01%	0.01%
2818	3054	80.94	34.82	37.74	1859	0.02%	0.02%	1876	0.02%	0.02%
2471	2288	80.52	30.68	28.41	1904	0.03%	0.04%	1919	0.03%	0.04%
3130	2668	82.25	38.05	32.44	1948	0.04%	0.07%	1963	0.03%	0.07%
2859	2417	81.53	35.06	29.64	1993	0.07%	0.10%	2006	0.10%	0.10%
2808	2726	82.81	33.91	32.92	2038	0.11%	0.16%	2050	0.11%	0.16%

The log-mean temperature difference, **LMTD**, and overall conductance (both hot and cold sides), Q_H and Q_C, are calculated as follows:

$$LMTD = \frac{\left(T_{H,in} - T_{C,out}\right) - \left(T_{H,out} - T_{C,in}\right)}{\ln\left(\dfrac{T_{H,in} - T_{C,out}}{T_{H,out} - T_{C,in}}\right)} \quad (4.3)$$

$$UA_H = \frac{Q_H}{LMTD} \quad (4.4)$$

$$UA_C = \frac{Q_C}{LMTD} \quad (4.5)$$

These quantities are listed in the spreadsheet as illustrated in the next figure. These are routine heat transfer calculations and may be found in any textbook on that subject. The span of values for each parameter is divided into fifty equal parts (or bins) and the number of occurrences of each value within each range is counted and divided by the total to arrive at percentages. An analytical model is included along side the Monte Carlo by way of comparison.

Each of the parameters, values, and corresponding columns in the spreadsheet is color-coded to help associated it with the graphs which follow. The calculations are only in the first three rows. After this the spreadsheet contains value. This is to speed up the calculations. It's still very slow to update. The values are filled in by pressing the button. All of the calculations are included in the spreadsheet. Press alt-F11 to open the VBA® window.

	LMTD			UAH			UAC	
0.66	stdev		3.46	stdev		3.45	stdev	
84.39	max		48.55	max	analy-	47.14	max	analy-
81.85	avg		34.21	avg	tical	34.37	avg	tical
79.17	min		20.49	min	model	20.88	min	model
79.27	0.00%	0.00%	21.05	0.00%	0.00%	21.41	0.00%	0.01%
79.37	0.01%	0.01%	21.61	0.00%	0.01%	21.93	0.00%	0.01%
79.48	0.00%	0.01%	22.18	0.01%	0.01%	22.46	0.02%	0.02%
79.58	0.01%	0.02%	22.74	0.02%	0.03%	22.98	0.01%	0.03%
79.69	0.02%	0.03%	23.30	0.03%	0.04%	23.51	0.04%	0.04%
79.79	0.03%	0.05%	23.86	0.04%	0.07%	24.03	0.05%	0.07%
79.90	0.08%	0.08%	24.42	0.07%	0.11%	24.56	0.08%	0.11%
80.00	0.13%	0.12%	24.98	0.12%	0.18%	25.08	0.12%	0.17%

The Monte Carlo simulation covers 65,525 cases which is sufficient granularity to result in remarkable agreement, as illustrated in the following figures:

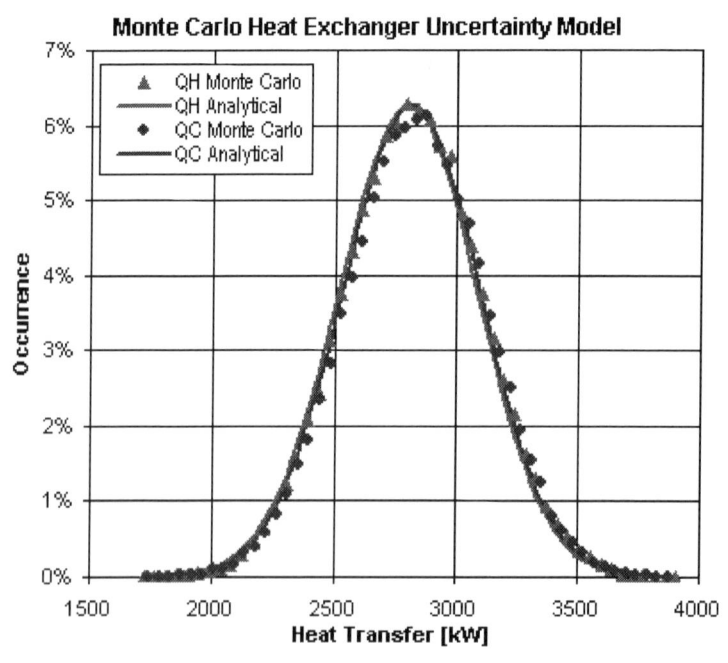

We might expect the heat transfer to exhibit this behavior. After all, it's just the product of two normally-distributed values times the difference in two more. We might not expect the LMTD and conductances to exhibit this behavior, as these involve division and a logarithm. However, these do, as illustrated in the next two figure:

20

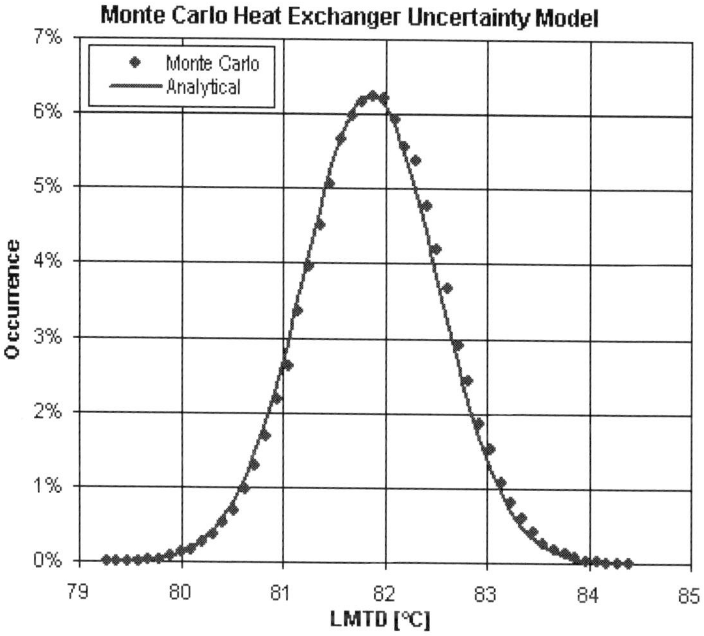
Monte Carlo Heat Exchanger Uncertainty Model
Monte Carlo
Analytical
Occurrence
0%
1%
2%
3%
4%
5%
6%
7%
79
80
81
82
83
84
85
LMTD [°C]

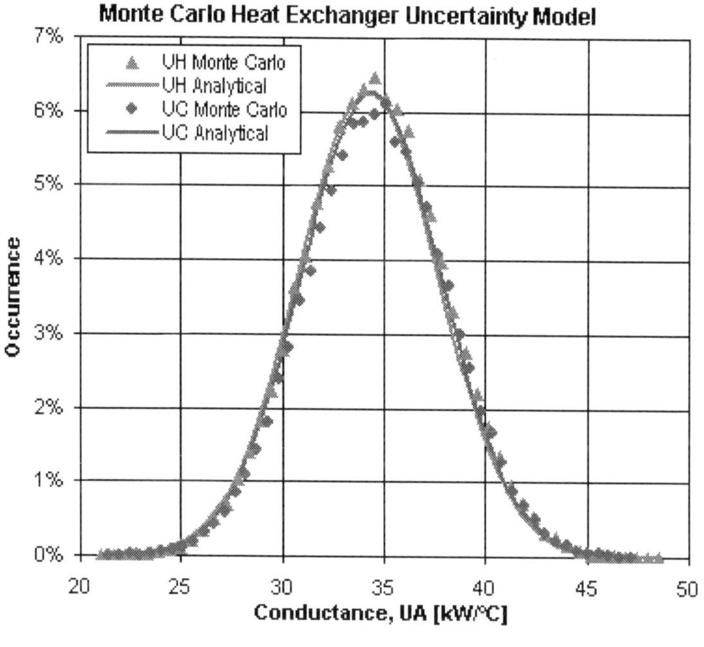
Monte Carlo Heat Exchanger Uncertainty Model
UH Monte Carlo
UH Analytical
UC Monte Carlo
UC Analytical
Occurrence
0%
1%
2%
3%
4%
5%
6%
7%
20
25
30
35
40
45
50
Conductance, UA [kW/°C]

Chapter 5. Log Normally-Distributed Parameters

We will next consider parameters that can be characterized by a log-normal distribution, that is, ones whose log exhibits a bell-shaped frequency distribution. While the previous parameters might take on any value (including positive, negative, and zero), log-normal parameters cannot. These never quite reach zero, can get quite large, and can't possibly be negative. Examples of common phenomena that may exhibit this behavior include: population growth rates, time to spread infectious diseases, and reaction response rates. We will begin with the last of these.

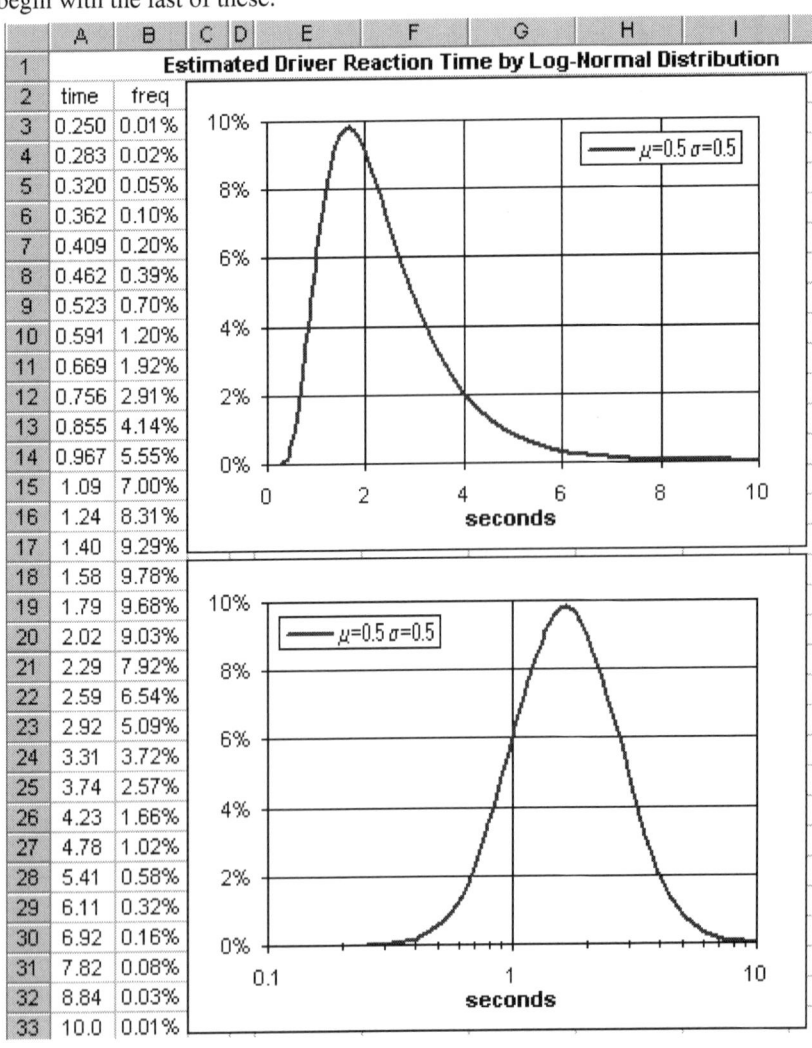

Estimated Driver Reaction Time by Log-Normal Distribution

time	freq
0.250	0.01%
0.283	0.02%
0.320	0.05%
0.362	0.10%
0.409	0.20%
0.462	0.39%
0.523	0.70%
0.591	1.20%
0.669	1.92%
0.756	2.91%
0.855	4.14%
0.967	5.55%
1.09	7.00%
1.24	8.31%
1.40	9.29%
1.58	9.78%
1.79	9.68%
2.02	9.03%
2.29	7.92%
2.59	6.54%
2.92	5.09%
3.31	3.72%
3.74	2.57%
4.23	1.66%
4.78	1.02%
5.41	0.58%
6.11	0.32%
6.92	0.16%
7.82	0.08%
8.84	0.03%
10.0	0.01%

Charts: $\mu=0.5\ \sigma=0.5$ (linear scale, seconds) and $\mu=0.5\ \sigma=0.5$ (log scale, seconds).

22

Drivers who are aware of their surroundings are often fascinated (and/or irritated) with the wide disparity in human reaction rates, especially in traffic. No driver exhibits a negative reaction rate, unless they possess precognition or are unconcerned with law enforcement and personal safety. Reaction rates of some drivers can be astonishingly long, depending on the number of mobile devices they're simultaneously interacting with, the movie playing on the little dashboard television, or perhaps the number of extraterrestrials they're communing with at the time.

The reaction rate of drivers can be roughly estimated by a log-normal distribution having both a mean and standard deviation of one-half ($\mu=0.5$ and $\sigma=0.5$), as illustrated in the previous figure. On row 3 we see that 1% (one out of a hundred) drivers have a reaction rate of 0.25 (1/4th) of a second. On the other end of the spectrum, on row 33 we see that 1% (one out of a hundred) drivers have a reaction time of 10 seconds. The log-normal distribution is obtained from Equations 1.1 and 1.2 by replacing x by $ln(x)$.

We can use this calculation as illustrated on the second tab of this spreadsheet to create the simplest traffic simulation in which cars are counted as passing through the intersection as long as the accumulated reaction time is less than or equal to the duration of the green.

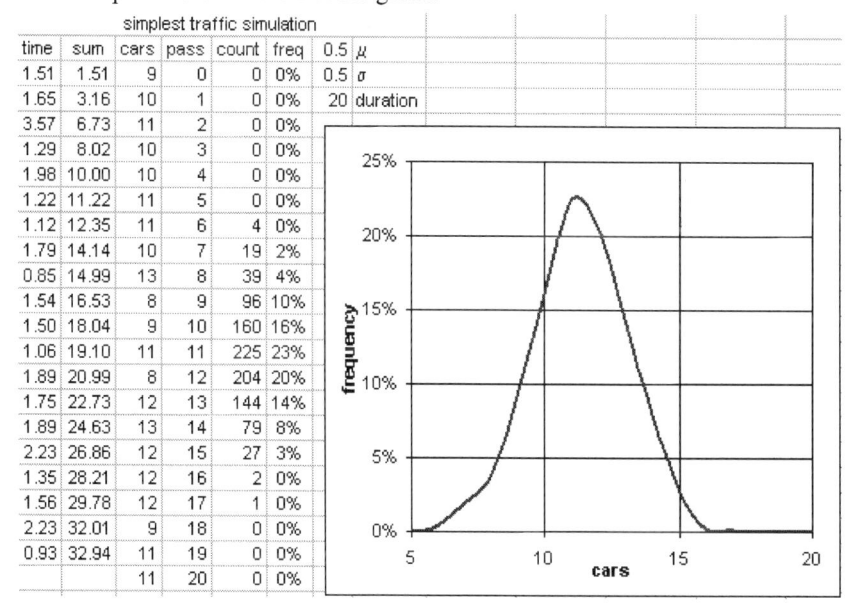

simplest traffic simulation

time	sum	cars	pass	count	freq	0.5	μ
1.51	1.51	9	0	0	0%	0.5	σ
1.65	3.16	10	1	0	0%	20	duration
3.57	6.73	11	2	0	0%		
1.29	8.02	10	3	0	0%		
1.98	10.00	10	4	0	0%		
1.22	11.22	11	5	0	0%		
1.12	12.35	11	6	4	0%		
1.79	14.14	10	7	19	2%		
0.85	14.99	13	8	39	4%		
1.54	16.53	8	9	96	10%		
1.50	18.04	9	10	160	16%		
1.06	19.10	11	11	225	23%		
1.89	20.99	8	12	204	20%		
1.75	22.73	12	13	144	14%		
1.89	24.63	13	14	79	8%		
2.23	26.86	12	15	27	3%		
1.35	28.21	12	16	2	0%		
1.56	29.78	12	17	1	0%		
2.23	32.01	9	18	0	0%		
0.93	32.94	11	19	0	0%		
		11	20	0	0%		

The first two columns illustrate the calculations. Column C (cars) contains 1000 simulated values. Columns D, E, and F calculate the statistics on column C, which is shown in the figure. For the parameters shown, on average 11 cars clear the intersection per cycle (225 out of 1000) with sometimes as few as 6 (4 out of 1000) and sometimes as many as 17 (1 out of 1000).

Chapter 6. Shuffling

Simulation of card games by Monte Carlo modeling is of very little value, as the odds are easily calculated. If the outcome is a surprise, then you programmed it wrong. Still, there are times when we went to *shuffle* lists of things such as cards. This is accomplished through random swapping. The spreadsheet shuffle.xls illustrates this.

	A	B	C	D	E	F	G	H	I	J	K	L	M	N
1	AS	KH	8H	4D	5C	5D	AS	1	26	21	30	44	31	1
2	2S	2D	QC	KD	5S	2S	QH	2	28	51	39	5	2	25
3	3S	3S	8S	KC	4C	KH	10C	3	3	8	52	43	26	49
4	4S	4S	3D	8H	KS	6C	4D	4	4	29	21	13	45	30
5	5S	8C	7D	2C	2H	9C	7D	5	47	33	41	15	48	33
6	6S	8S	6S	6C	QH	4H	QC	6	8	6	45	25	17	51
7	7S	7S	9D	10C	3C	2C	QS	7	7	35	49	42	41	12
8	8S	7C	3C	JS	JS	KS	7H	8	46	42	11	11	13	20
9	9S	9S	10S	4H	7H	KD	4S	9	9	10	17	20	39	4
10	10S	10S	QD	JC	9H	10S	KH	10	10	38	50	22	10	26
11	JS	JS	2C	8S	10S	9H	10D	11	11	41	8	10	22	36
12	QS	QS	QS	8C	6H	QS	9S	12	12	12	47	19	12	9
13	KS	KS	6H	JD	QC	4S	5S	13	13	19	37	51	4	5
14	AH	AH	KS	2D	3S	5S	KC	14	14	13	28	3	5	52
15	2H	2H	JS	2H	6C	3C	8C	15	15	11	15	45	42	47

The cards in column A are in order. The cards in columns B through G have been shuffled by randomly swapping the indices (1 through 52) in columns I through N. There's a button to update the shuffling. Column I is has 26 swaps, J has 52 swaps, K has 78 swaps, and so forth through column N with 156 swaps. The adequacy of shuffling is illustrated in this next figure:

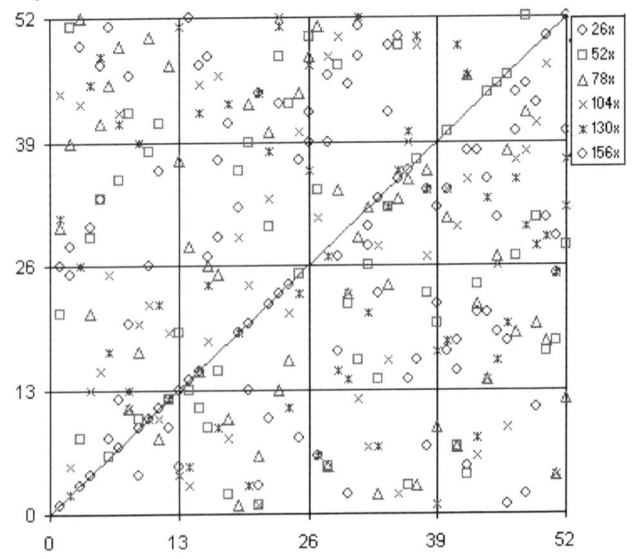

24

Many of the blue diamonds and some of the magenta squares lie on the black line, indicating insufficient shuffling, Linear regression on the red triangles results in a negative (downward) slope and an R^2 of 0.0691. This is the bare minimum number of random swaps to achieve meaningful shuffling.

Clearly, we need to develop some measures of adequacy for shuffling. For illustration, we will return to the slot machine. There are 21 pictures on each reel with the number of pictures slightly different. The simplest measure of adequate shuffling in this case is the minimum distance between any two of the same thing. We must consider both forward and backward or wrap-around on the reel. This is easily accomplished by using the remainder of the index and 21 (the total number of pictures). The code listed in Appendix D shuffles the pictures on the reel and keeps the result with the highest score. There's no point continuing after reaching the maximum score of 4, thus the statement if(j>3)break. This code utilizes string comparisons (strcmp()==0), but integers would be considerably faster. The output is as follows:

```
bar    bar    bar
cherry plum   orange
orange bell   lemon
bell   orange bell
plum   lemon  plum
bar    bar    orange
cherry cherry cherry
lemon  plum   bell
bell   bell   lemon
plum   orange orange
orange lemon  plum
lemon  cherry lemon
bell   plum   cherry
plum   bell   orange
orange orange lemon
cherry lemon  bell
lemon  plum   orange
bar    bell   lemon
orange orange bell
bell   lemon  plum
lemon  cherry lemon
4      4      3
```

A method of scoring to measure the effectiveness of shuffling a deck of cards might be to look for runs and pairs. A run of four would be better than three (worse shuffling). Three of a kind would be better than two (also worse shuffling). One obvious way would be to apply poker machine payback rates to the various combinations and then compare scores, with the intent to achieve the minimum score. The code listed in Appendix E simulates this process. The output looks like this:

```
initializing deck
AS  2S  3S  4S  5S  6S  7S  8S  9S  10S JS  QS  KS
AH  2H  3H  4H  5H  6H  7H  8H  9H  10H JH  QH  KH
AD  2D  3D  4D  5D  6D  7D  8D  9D  10D JD  QD  KD
AC  2C  3C  4C  5C  6C  7C  8C  9C  10C JC  QC  KC
score=15635080025945000800000
shuffling deck (26 swaps)
AS  10C JC  8C  6H  6S  4C  3C  9S  3H  9D  QS  KS
QD  7D  7S  4H  5S  5H  7H  8D  9H  10H 4D  AD  KH
QH  2D  5C  JH  KD  2H  10S 8H  AH  10D 7C  6D  5D
JS  2C  8S  AC  3D  9C  JD  4S  KC  3S  2S  QC  6C
score=2664
shuffling deck (26 swaps)
AS  10C 7H  8C  6H  4C  2S  3C  10H 3H  7S  5H  QC
QD  7D  5S  4H  JS  QS  KS  8D  KD  5D  4D  9H  AH
5C  2D  AD  JH  KH  2H  JC  8H  9D  10D 7C  6D  9S
6S  2C  AC  8S  QH  3D  JD  4S  3S  KC  9C  10S 6C
score=3150
shuffling deck (26 swaps)
AS  3S  7H  8C  6H  KH  10S 3C  10H 8D  7S  2H  QC
AD  5C  QD  6S  KD  AC  KS  3H  9D  5D  4D  2D  9C
9S  2C  10C QS  7D  5H  JC  KC  JS  6D  7C  10D 5S
4H  JH  9H  QH  8S  3D  JD  4S  4C  8H  AH  2S  6C
score=125
shuffling deck (26 swaps)
KS  4D  8H  8C  6H  QC  10S 6C  6D  2D  7H  2H  3D
4S  AD  QH  6S  KD  AC  4C  KH  AH  4H  QS  8D  9C
9S  2C  10C 3S  7D  5C  JC  KC  JS  7C  9D  2S  5S
5D  JH  9H  QD  8S  10D JD  7S  AS  3C  10H 3H  5H
score=250
shuffling deck (26 swaps)
KS  4D  8C  6D  6H  QC  2C  6C  8H  2D  7H  2H  10C
KC  JH  QH  6S  AD  10S 9S  4C  AC  4H  10H 8D  8S
9D  5H  JC  3S  JS  3H  3D  4S  JD  3C  QD  5C  5D
5S  7C  AH  KD  9C  10D 7D  7S  AS  KH  QS  2S  9H
score=188
```

The score drops off very sharply with each pair of cards swapped, as illustrated in this next figure for four different initial random number seeds:

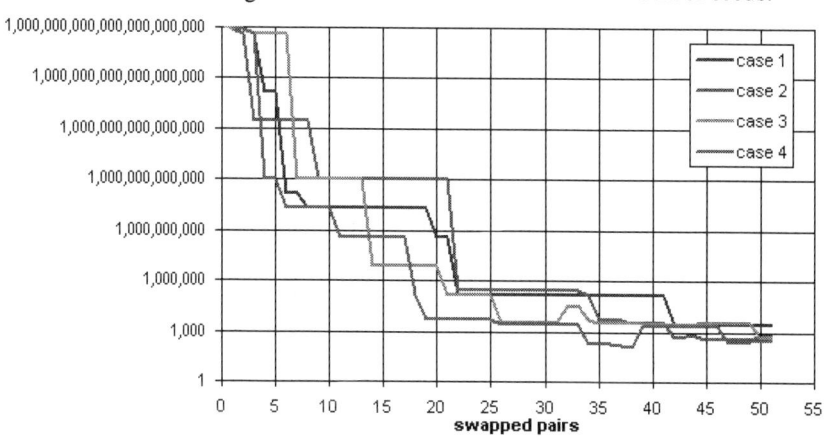

Chapter 7. Sampling

In this chapter we will consider one type of sampling problem: a process exists and is well behaved, but we can't continuously or exhaustively measure or calculate it. This situation arises in practice for several reasons, including: 1) it's too expensive or takes too long to measure continuously, 2) it isn't possible with available instrumentation to measure precisely, 3) the process of measuring disturbs the process and we want to disrupt it as little as possible.

The first of these problems arises whenever people are involved. You can interview people on the street, exiting the polls, or through mass mailings, but you'll never get to the end of the matter. The second of these problems is always the case with instruments measuring temperature, pressure, voltage, current, and pretty much everything else. The third problem arises with living things, whether you're trying to raise pigs or culture the latest communicable disease.

In this first example, we pick two random values within some range (-180 to +180 and -90 to plus 90) as our sampling points and apply some test or calculation (in this case inside polygon?). After 10,000 points, a pattern clearly emerges:

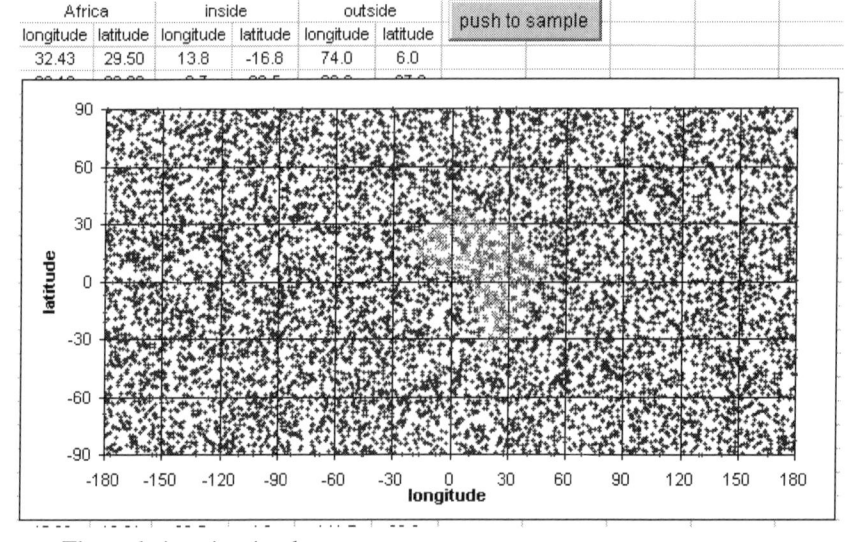

Africa		inside		outside		push to sample
longitude	latitude	longitude	latitude	longitude	latitude	
32.43	29.50	13.8	-16.8	74.0	6.0	

The code is quite simple:

```
For i = 1 To 10000
   lon = -180 + 360 * Rnd()
   lat = -90 + 180 * Rnd()
   If (InsidePolygon(Range("A3:A221"),
Range("B3:B221"), lon, lat)) Then
      irow = irow + 1
      Cells(irow, 3).Value = lon
      Cells(irow, 4).Value = lat
```

```
    Else
      jrow = jrow + 1
      Cells(jrow, 5).Value = lon
      Cells(jrow, 6).Value = lat
    End If
  Next i
```

Next we will consider actual instrument readings taken during a performance test of a large steam surface condenser (condenser_data.xls). The pressure sensor was read and the value recorded at 30-second intervals for approximately 11 hours. This is what the data looks like for pressure vs. time.

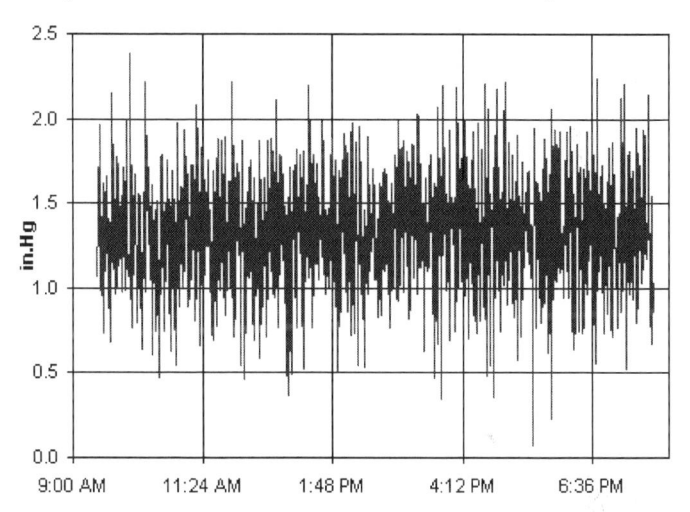

While this data might look scruffy, it is not. In fact, this data set is idyllic. The frequency of occurrence of the values is shown in this next figure:

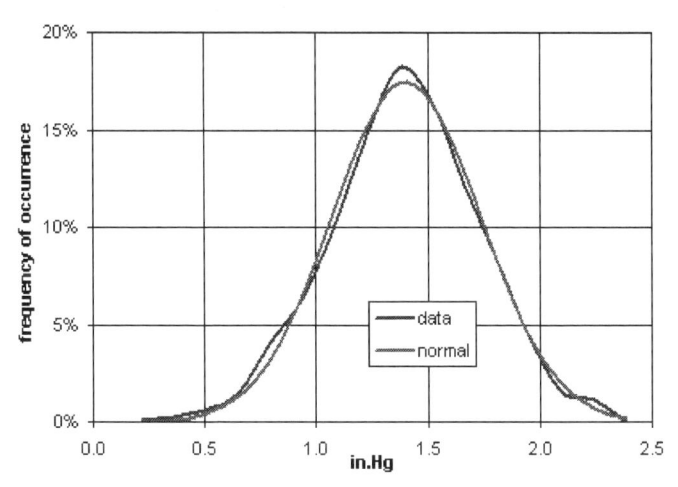

29

You couldn't ask for better agreement between actual data and the normal distribution. I had to search through a lot of test data to find a set so very nearly perfect in the statistical sense. This same data on the following day is shown in this next figure:

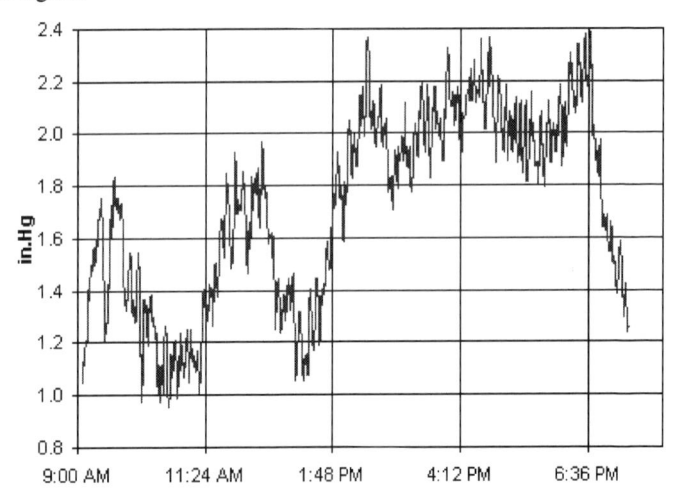

The frequency of occurrence of this second day's data is shown below:

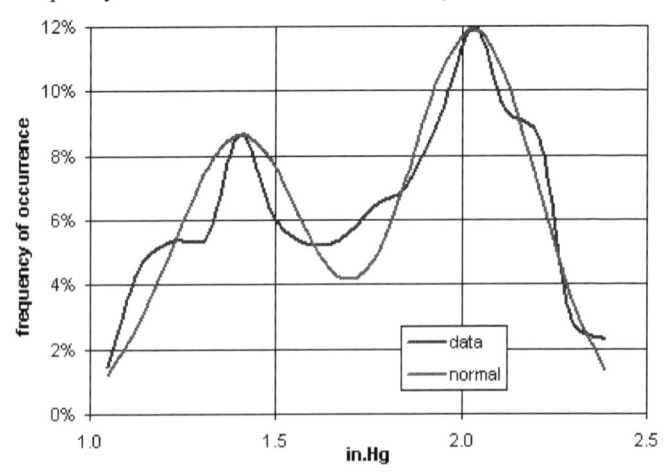

This second set of data very nearly fits a double-humped normal distribution (i.e., the weighted sum of two normal distributions). We will see how to model distributions like this in the next chapter. The two means are the two peaks (1.404 and 2.030). The two weights are the relative heights of the two peaks (43% and 57%). The two standard deviations are proportional to the widths of the humps (0.181 and 0.172).

We will next consider actual solar data collected at 30-second intervals from 142 instruments spread out over approximately 500 acres. Three days have been selected from a larger data set to illustrate clear, average, and cloudy conditions. The following graph shows direct normal insolation (DNI) over time.

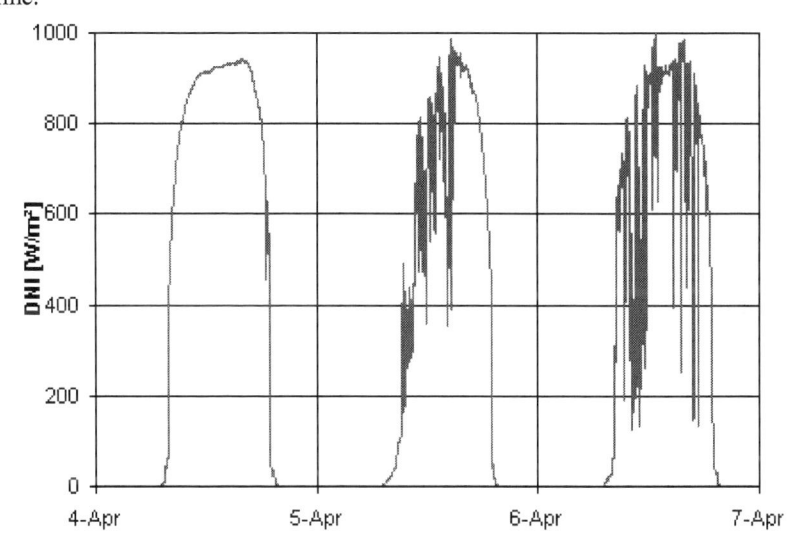

The distribution of values over these three days is shown in this next figure:

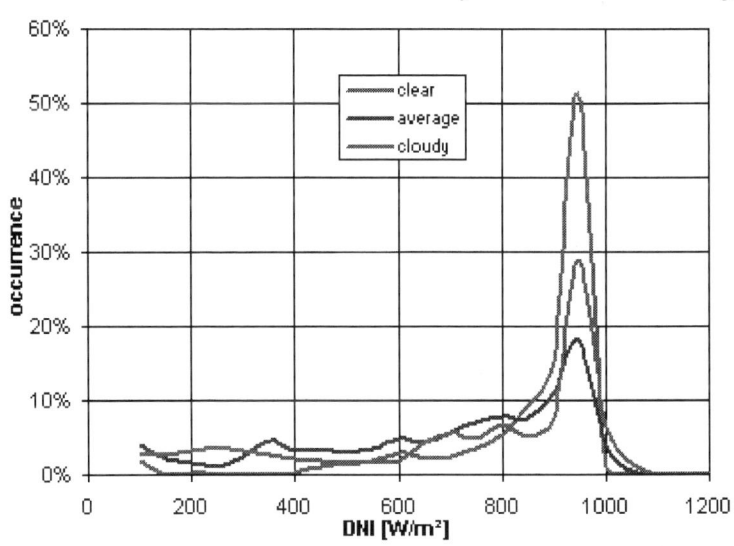

The area under each curve is the same (i.e., 100%). The peaks occur at nearly the same level (approximately 950), as this is what the sensors see when there isn't a cloud shading them from the sun. Clearly, the standard bell-shaped curve of the normal or log-normal will suffice for this data. What we need in this case is a coordinate (or variable) transformation.

We will not consider the clear day data in more depth. First, we eliminate the pre-dawn and post-sunset data. This narrows the window of time from 7:51 AM to 6:54 PM and leaves 664 30-second time intervals, each with 142 instrument readings. The distribution for this limited data set is shown in the following figure:

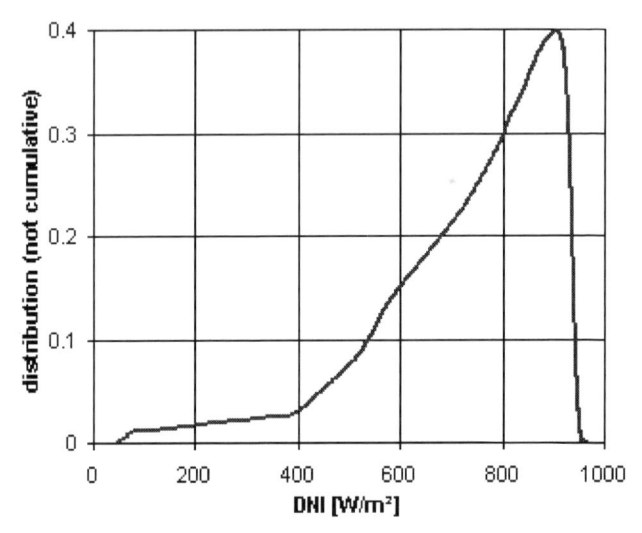

We next take the remaining 94,288 data points and sort them in increasing order. By adding the row number this gives us a list of DNI vs. number of points. Dividing the number of points by the total yields the cumulative probability. We can shorten this list without losing any information by eliminating sequential rows with the same value of DNI. You will find this list in solar_transform.xls columns ES through EU.

As this represents cumulative probability, we can use the Excel® function NORMSINV() to get the equivalent $z=(x-\mu)/\sigma$ in column EV. We can use this to get the density f=NORMDIST(z,0,1,FALSE) in column EW. We can then use this to produce random numbers that have the exact same probability as the data. Push the button to generate 65,534 normally-distributed random numbers ($\mu=0$, $\sigma=1$) in column EX. Next, use these random numbers to look up (linearly interpolate) a corresponding value of DNI to go in column EY. The statistics for this fabricated data are in columns EZ through FB. The cumulative probability of the fabricated data (red +s) is so close to the actual data (blue curve) that it's hard to see the curve.

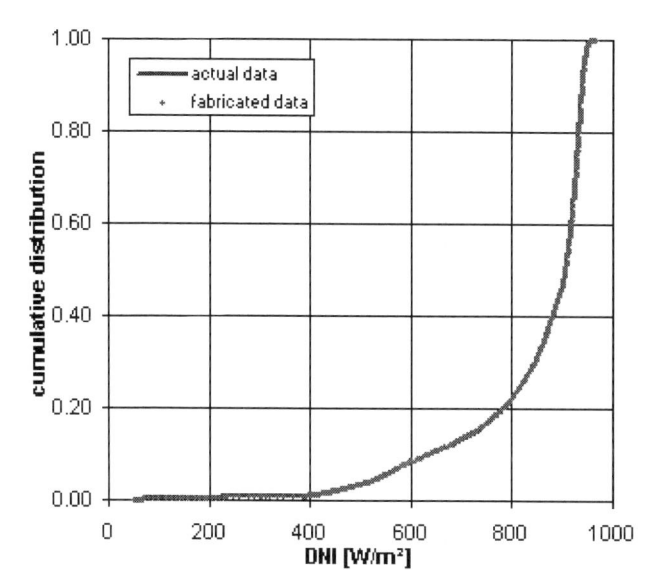

[Figure: Cumulative distribution vs DNI [W/m²], showing actual data and fabricated data]

You can just barely see it near the bottom axis between 200 and 400. While this is generating random data the hard way, it may necessary in order to accurately characterize a process that doesn't fit the usual bell-shaped distribution curve. We will consider a different type of sampling in Chapter 13.

Chapter 8. Systematic Bias

As we saw in the last chapter, some things exhibit more than one hump. This is evidence of systematic bias. In the case of the condenser data this arose from a subtle change in operation. Systematic bias can be modeled using two means and two standard deviations plus a switch. If the two are equally likely, a 0/1 switch is adequate and is easily implemented by testing the remainder with 2, which is always 0 or 1. For an unevenly split bias, simply compare a random number to some threshold.

The following figure uses a heat exchanger calculation to illustrate no bias, uncorrelated bias and correlated bias. The code to produce this is listed in Appendix F.

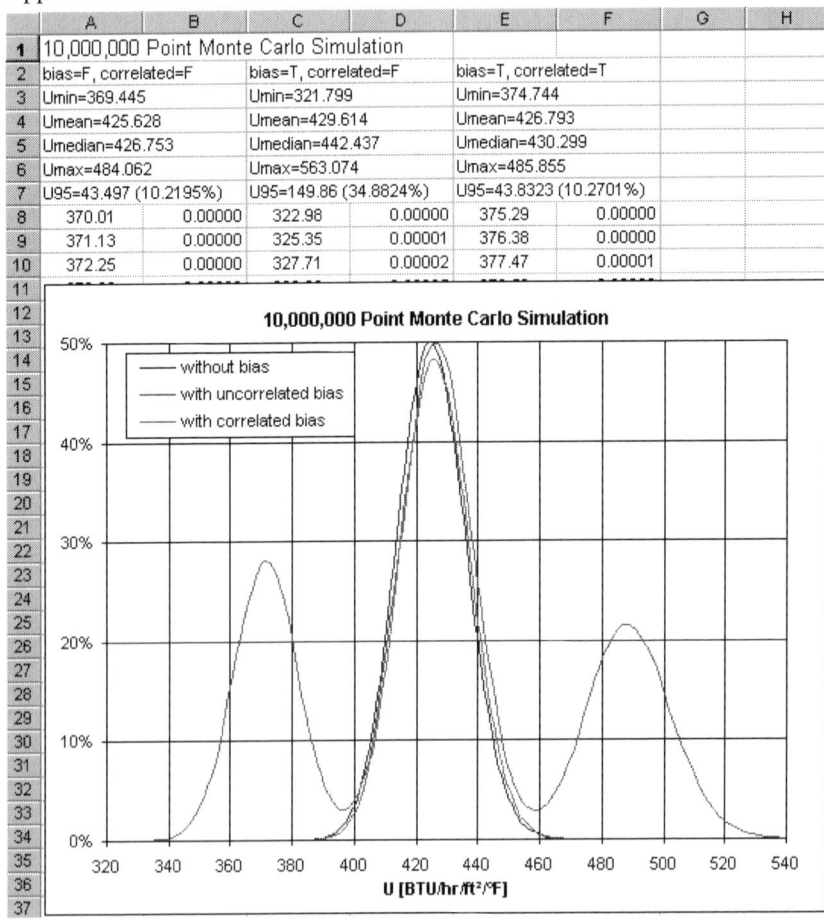

	A	B	C	D	E	F	G	H
1	10,000,000 Point Monte Carlo Simulation							
2	bias=F, correlated=F		bias=T, correlated=F		bias=T, correlated=T			
3	Umin=369.445		Umin=321.799		Umin=374.744			
4	Umean=425.628		Umean=429.614		Umean=426.793			
5	Umedian=426.753		Umedian=442.437		Umedian=430.299			
6	Umax=484.062		Umax=563.074		Umax=485.855			
7	U95=43.497 (10.2195%)		U95=149.86 (34.8824%)		U95=43.8323 (10.2701%)			
8	370.01	0.00000	322.98	0.00000	375.29	0.00000		
9	371.13	0.00000	325.35	0.00001	376.38	0.00000		
10	372.25	0.00000	327.71	0.00002	377.47	0.00001		

10,000,000 Point Monte Carlo Simulation

— without bias
— with uncorrelated bias
— with correlated bias

U [BTU/hr·ft²/°F]

The figure in the previous chapter with the blue and red curves exhibiting two humps shows correlated bias, as a shift in the data arises from an

34

operational decision. The data either come before or after the decision was made. In this case before is analogous to zero and after is analogous to one. We can easily generate random data that exhibits this same statistical behavior. This calculation illustrates two things, the dual mean/standard deviation plus the threshold. The code that performs this is in the spreadsheet and listed below:

```
If (Rnd() < r) Then
    Cells(i, 9).Value = ndist(m1, s1)
Else
    Cells(i, 9).Value = ndist(m2, s2)
End If
```

Push the button to create 65,535 such random values, compile the statistics as before, and draw the result on top of the previous graph and the red dots lie right on top of the red curve:

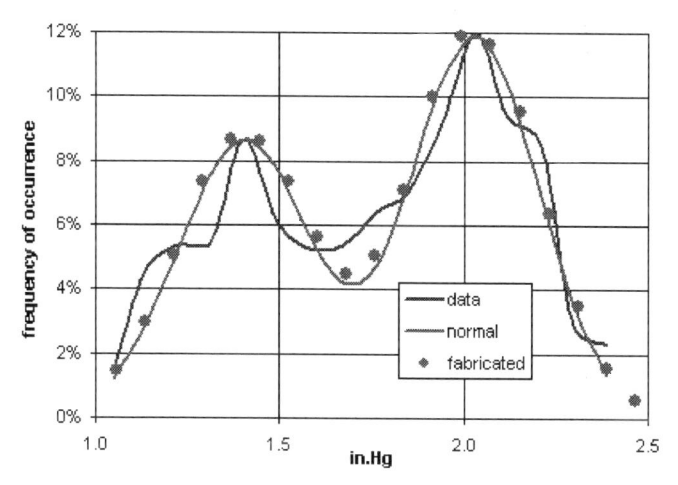

If the instruments used to collect this data were calibrated in the same way to the same standard, the bias will be correlated (i.e., they all read consistently high or they all read consistently low). If they were calibrated in different ways, different times, or to different standards, this would not be true. This is how correlated bias is distinguished from uncorrelated.

The following is Figure 4-2-1 in ASME PTC 19.1-2013[1], which illustrates the relationship between systematic error (or bias), random error, and total error. The systematic error is often overlooked, yet can exceed the random error in magnitude. PTC 19.1, "Test Uncertainty," contains further discussion on this subject.

---

[1] Image used in accordance with federal copyright (fair use doctrine) law. Usage does not imply endorsement of copyright holder (© 2013 American Society of Mechanical Engineers).

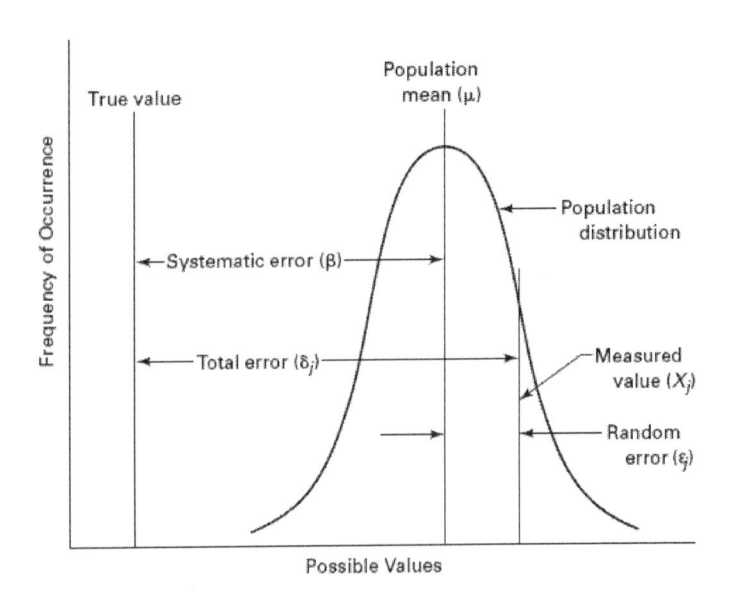

Chapter 9. Traffic

We now have all the tools to develop a more realistic traffic simulation. The number of cars making it through the green was introduced in Chapter 6 after describing how driver reaction times could be estimated by a log-normal distribution. The rate of traffic arrival is definitely biased. We expect a hump in the morning and another one in the evening due to work schedules. Two-humped distributions were introduced in Chapter 8. We can combine these to create a more realistic simulation.

According to the Department of Transportation Traffic Signal Timing Manual, there is something called the "minimum green needed to satisfy driver expectancy." Don't you just love it? Translation: If you make it any longer people fuss. There are tables of such values in Chapter 5 of the DOT TSTM. There are also tables of "minimum green needed to satisfy queue clearance." Translation: If you make it any shorter people fuss.

You will find the simulation in traffic.xls:

	A	B	C	D	E	F	G	H	I	J	K	L
1		Simulated Car Arrival Rate					arrival	reaction	cars	rate	reaction	freq
2	12:30 AM	9	0	mean	rate	stdev	12:35 AM	2.00	1	8	0.16	
3	1:30 AM	14	12	7:30 AM	25	0.02	12:39 AM	1.41	2	14	0.18	1
4	2:30 AM	23	30	12:30 PM	100	0.2	12:40 AM	3.12	3	19	0.22	0
5	3:30 AM	34	59	5:30 PM	25	0.02	12:44 AM	2.80	4	36	0.26	0
6	4:30 AM	50	101				12:46 AM	1.74	5	50	0.31	1
7	5:30 AM	69	160		cars		12:46 AM	2.07	6	72	0.37	2
8	6:30 AM	148	269				12:51 AM	0.86	7	198	0.44	3
9	7:30 AM	615	650	driver reaction rate			12:57 AM	1.25	8	554	0.52	18
10	8:30 AM	198	1057	0.5	μ		1:09 AM	3.04	9	243	0.61	50
11	9:30 AM	164	1238	0.5	σ		1:11 AM	1.42	10	151	0.73	107
12	10:30 AM	183	1411	20	duration		1:15 AM	1.41	11	179	0.87	179
13	11:30 AM	195	1600				1:18 AM	1.25	12	199	1.03	265
14	12:30 PM	199	1797				1:25 AM	2.23	13	210	1.22	343
15	1:30 PM	195	1995				1:27 AM	2.69	14	172	1.45	438
16	2:30 PM	183	2184				1:33 AM	2.27	15	196	1.73	490
17	3:30 PM	164	2357				1:36 AM	1.43	16	173	2.05	460
18	4:30 PM	198	2538				1:37 AM	0.67	17	209	2.43	386
19	5:30 PM	615	2945				1:44 AM	0.85	18	523	2.89	339
20	6:30 PM	148	3326				1:52 AM	0.81	19	186	3.43	230
21	7:30 PM	69	3435				1:53 AM	1.42	20	65	4.08	141
22	8:30 PM	50	3494				1:54 AM	1.76	21	50	4.84	62
23	9:30 PM	34	3536				1:57 AM	2.05	22	39	5.75	40
24	10:30 PM	23	3565				2:03 AM	1.63	23	19	6.83	18
25	11:30 PM	14	3583				2:04 AM	1.48	24	18	8.12	8
26							2:04 AM	0.99	25	3583	9.64	1
27							2:05 AM	1.68	26		11.45	1
28							2:18 AM	0.80	27			3583

We will first create a distribution to characterize the rate of arrivals. Because a few cars pass through our simulated intersection all night long, we

37

will begin with a very wide low hump. We will then two steeper humps at 7:30 AM and 5:30 PM. The resulting distribution is shown below:

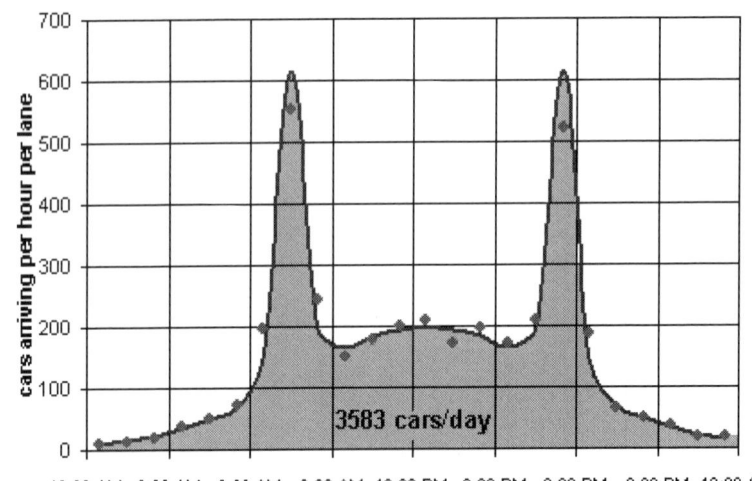

[Graph: cars arriving per hour per lane vs time of day, showing 3583 cars/day with peaks at 7:30 AM and 5:30 PM]

The area under the curve is the number of cars/day/lane, which is 3583. We create 3583 cars at various times and then sort them to produce random arrival times that result in this distribution (as shown by the red dots). The cumulative number of cars arriving at the intersection is shown in this next figure:

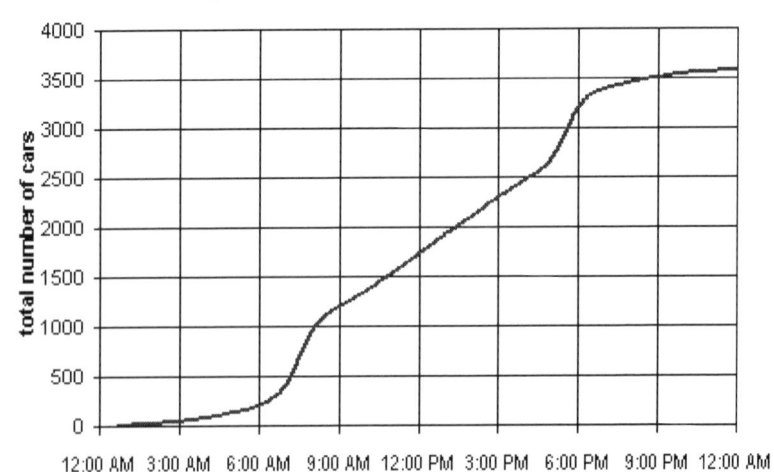

[Graph: total number of cars vs time of day, cumulative curve reaching ~3583]

We also create a reaction time for each driver (as before using $\mu=0.5$ and $\sigma=0.5$ seconds log-normal distribution). We now have a list of cars, each with a driver and a reaction time. The distribution of reaction times is shown in this next figure:

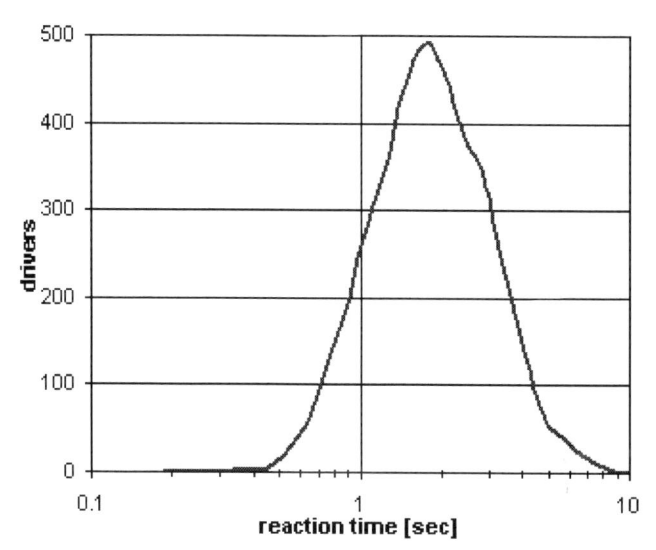

The code to create cars and driver reaction time is very simple:

```
While (i < n)
  r = Rnd()
  If (r <= r1 / (r1 + r2 + r3)) Then
     t = ndist(t1, s1)
  ElseIf (r <= (r1 + r2) / (r1 + r2 + r3)) Then
     t = ndist(t2, s2)
  Else
     t = ndist(t3, s3)
  End If
  If (t >= t0 And t < t0 + 1) Then
     i = i + 1
     Cells(i + 1, 7).Value = t
     Cells(i + 1, 8).Value = Exp(ndist(mu, sigma))
  End If
Wend
```

Rates r1, r2, and r3 correspond to the morning, continuous, and evening surges in traffic (25, 100, 25). Times t1, t2, and t3 are the means of these three rates (7:30 AM, 12:30 PM, and 5:30 PM). Standard deviations s1, s2, and s3 correspond to these same three surges. Driver reaction is calculated from *exp(τ)* where τ is calculated from μ and σ.

All we have to do now is select an interval for the traffic light and advance through time to see how many cars get through per sequence throughout the day and how many cars queue up during the peak times. Perform this simulation with Excel® requires a slight modification. We must recalculate the driver reaction every time we check for whether a car can make it through the light or not. Without this modification we would need a growing queue of cars waiting, each with a different reaction time. Allocation of arrays in Excel® is a disaster. Don't even try it. The resulting code is rather simple:

```
Function simulation(this_time As Double, cars_wait As
    Integer, prev_cycle As Integer, _
  mu_react As Double, sigma_react As Double, green_dura
    As Double, yellow_dura As Double) As Variant
  Dim seconds As Double, begin As Double, this_dura As
    Double, this_cycle As Integer, this_react As Double
  seconds = 24# * 3600# * (this_time - Int(this_time))
  this_cycle = Int(seconds / (2# * (green_dura +
    yellow_dura)))
  this_dura = green_dura
  While (this_cycle > prev_cycle + 1 And cars_wait > 0)
    this_react = Exp(ndist(mu_react, sigma_react))
    If (this_dura >= this_react) Then
      cars_wait = cars_wait - 1
      this_dura = this_dura - this_react
    Else
      this_dura = green_dura
      prev_cycle = prev_cycle + 1
    End If
  Wend
  begin = 2# * (green_dura + yellow_dura) * Int(seconds
    / (2# * (green_dura + yellow_dura)))
  this_dura = seconds - begin
  this_react = Exp(ndist(mu_react, sigma_react))
  If (this_dura < this_react) Then
    cars_wait = cars_wait + 1
  End If
  simulation = Array(cars_wait, this_cycle)
End Function
```

We first check if the light changed since the last time we called the function (this cycle greater than previous cycle plus one). If so, then we pass cars through (each with it's own reaction time) until the light expires and the number of cycles catches up to the current. Then we either pass this car or add it to the queue if there's isn't enough time left on the green. Here's the result:

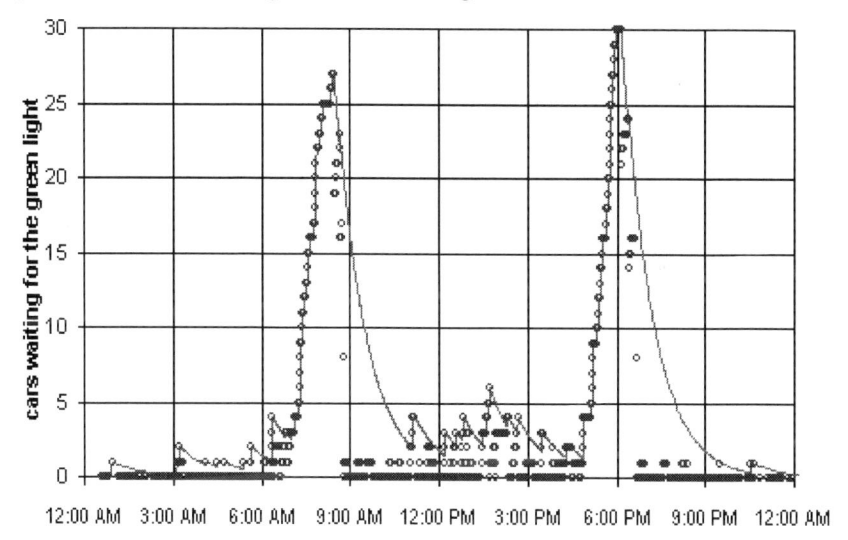

Chapter 10. Solar Collectors

We will next consider a solar collector simulation. First, we will create a cloud cover simulation to illustrate how clouds impact a field of solar collectors. The impact of clouds and haze on solar collector power output is much larger than most people are aware. The animation along with the program to create it may be found in the "clouds" folder of the on-line archive. The first frame of the animation is shown below:

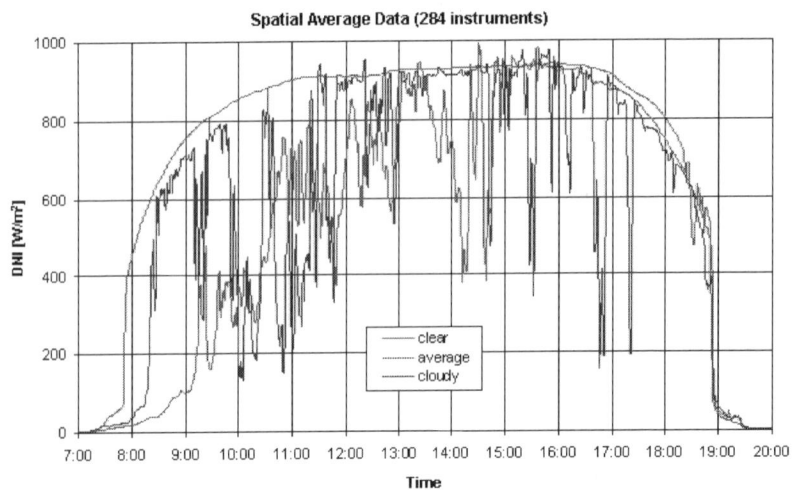

The previous figure shows the average of 284 instruments spread out over the entire solar field. The red curve represents the maximum available power for a given time of day. The area under this curve is the maximum available energy for the entire day. The area between the red and blue or green curves represents the amount of energy in that day which doesn't make it to the collectors and can't be converted to electricity. The variability for a single instrument is shown in this next figure, which is more representative of a single solar collector.

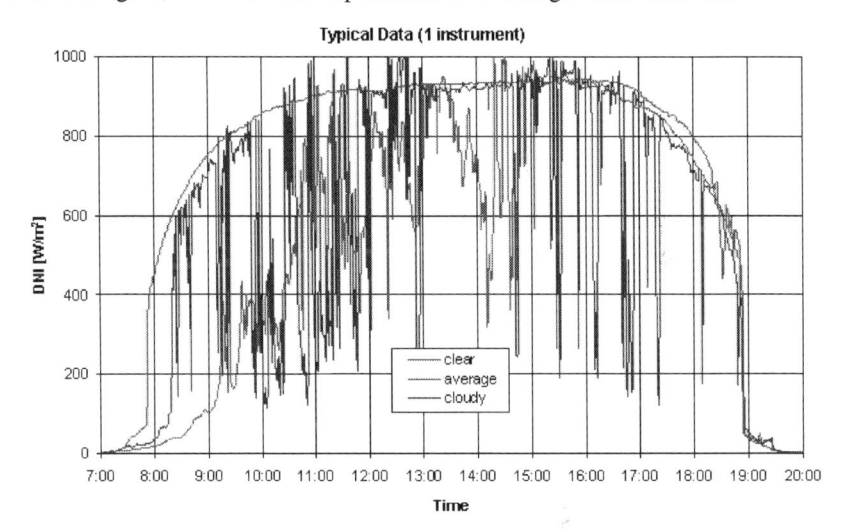

Typical Data (1 instrument)

The human eye is not the best indicator of incoming solar energy. What may seem bright and clear to humans as a matter of opinion doesn't necessarily correspond to power arriving at solar cells. Not only do clouds impact the incoming sunlight, but haze has a strong impact too. The measured cloudiness over Phoenix, a location known for its clear skies, is shown in this next figure:

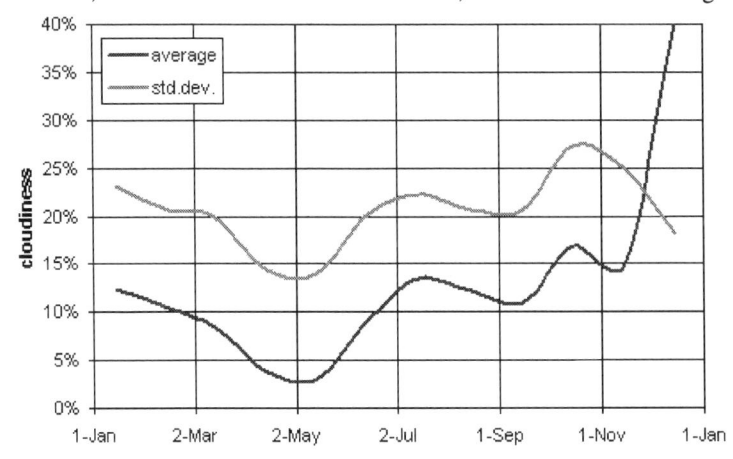

43

The standard deviation for 11 months out of the year exceeds the average, which is a problem if we're trying to create a Monte Carlo simulation. Just as in the case of driver reaction presented in Chapter 5, we will first consider the probability density of the natural log of the cloudiness:

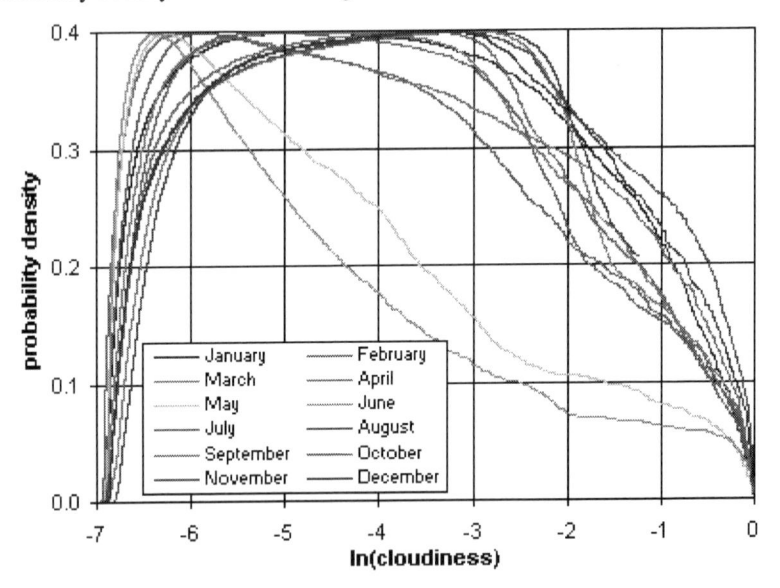

These clearly don't follow the log-normal distribution curve. This next figure shows the average and standard deviation of the natural log of the cloudiness per month:

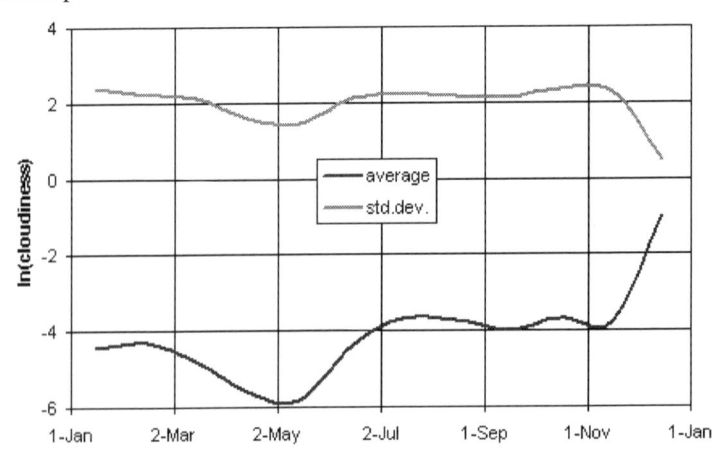

The fact that the distribution of cloudiness doesn't follow any of the basic shapes leads us to yet another way of modeling the behavior: randomly select the value from a known list using a uniformly-distributed random number. This

44

process requires a lot of data, but guarantees that we will replicate the expected behavior. The code to accomplish this simulation is rather short:

```
Private Sub CommandButton1_Click()
  Dim d As Long, h As Integer, da As Double, lat As
    Double, lon As Double, clr As Double
  Dim day As Date, mo As Integer, nd As Integer, id As
    Integer, gen As Double, i As Integer
  Dim cloudiness As Double, mn As Integer
  lat = Worksheets("Sheet1").Range("D1").Value
  lon = Worksheets("Sheet1").Range("F1").Value
  i = 2
  For d = 43101 To 46753
    gen = 0#
    For h = 1 To 24
      For mn = 1 To 60
        da = d + ((mn - 0.5) / 60 + (h - 0.5)) / 24#
        day = da
        clr = DNIclear(lat, lon, day)
        If (clr > 0) Then
          mo = month(day)
          nd = Worksheets("Sheet1").Cells(2, 8 + 2 * mo).Value
          id = (irand() Mod nd) + 3
          cloudiness = Exp(Worksheets("Sheet1").Cells(id, 8 + 2 * mo).Value)
          gen = gen + clr * (1# - cloudiness) / 60#
        End If
      Next mn
    Next h
    i = i + 1
    Cells(i, 1).Select
    Cells(i, 1).Value = d + 0.5
    Cells(i, 2).Value = gen
  Next d
End Sub
```

Loops are used to step through 10 years by day, then by hour, and finally by minute. The clear sky DNI is calculated from the NREL's Solar Position Algorithm.[2] A random index for the month is created and then used to fetch a cloudiness. The cloudiness is combined with the clear sky DNI to arrive at a maximum possible solar collector output per unit area. This solar collector output is accumulated over the day and the total written back onto the sheet next to the date.

---

[2] Reda, I. and Andreas, A., "Solar Position Algorithm for Solar Radiation Applications," National Renewable Energy Laboratory Report No. TP-560-34302, pp. 55, 2003, revised January 2008.

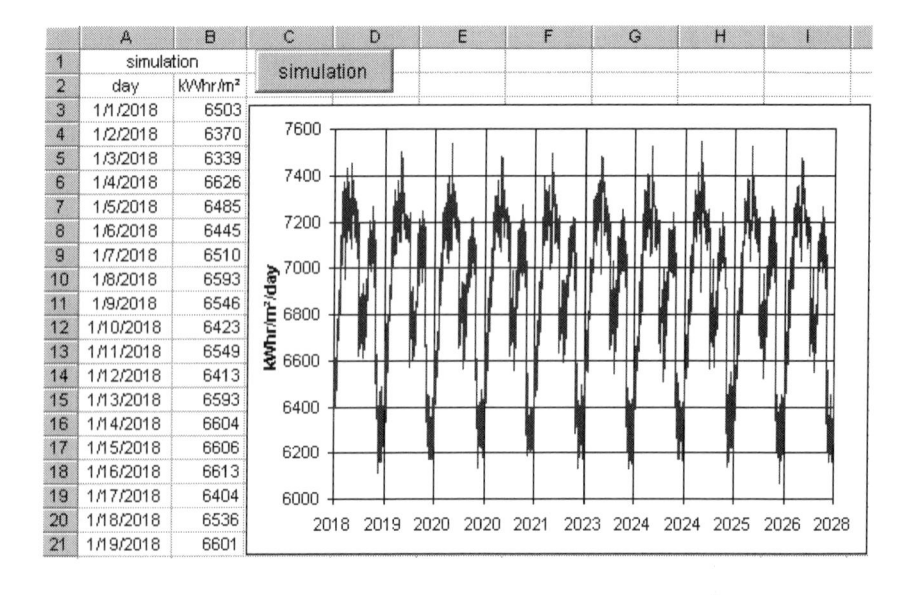

day	kWhr/m²
1/1/2018	6503
1/2/2018	6370
1/3/2018	6339
1/4/2018	6626
1/5/2018	6485
1/6/2018	6445
1/7/2018	6510
1/8/2018	6593
1/9/2018	6546
1/10/2018	6423
1/11/2018	6549
1/12/2018	6413
1/13/2018	6593
1/14/2018	6604
1/15/2018	6606
1/16/2018	6613
1/17/2018	6404
1/18/2018	6536
1/19/2018	6601

Chapter 11. Random Walk

Random walks are often presented in the context of Monte Carlo simulations. Unless you have some specific interest in modeling the behavior of drunkards, these may seem superfluous. There are useful applications of the random walk concept, so we'll just start with one of these: diffusion. To illustrate this we will employ a simple Windows® program. All it does is draw a cluster of yellow dots on a black background. The dots are subjected to diffusion *rattling* so that they spread over time, as illustrated below:

The code to *rattle* the particles is simple:
```
GetClientRect(hMain,&rc);
for(p=0;p<particles;p++)
    {
    r=1+rand()%20;
    a=rand()%360;
    u=nint(r*cos(M_PI*a/180.));
    v=nint(r*sin(M_PI*a/180.));
    Particle[p].x=max(0,min(rc.right-
1,Particle[p].x+u));
    Particle[p].y=max(0,min(rc.bottom-
1,Particle[p].y+v));
    }
```
Each particle is moved some random distance (1 to 20) at some random angle (0 to 359°). The positions are clamped to the edges of the window. The entire code is listed in Appendix G. This method has been used with remarkable

success to model contaminant transport. Several illustrations and animations may be seen at this location
http://dudleybenton.altervista.org/projects/Ptrax/ParticleTracking.html

An extensive comparison has been made between the analytical solution and the numerical one, which utilizes this random walk. This next figure shows the results after 15 years simulation time:

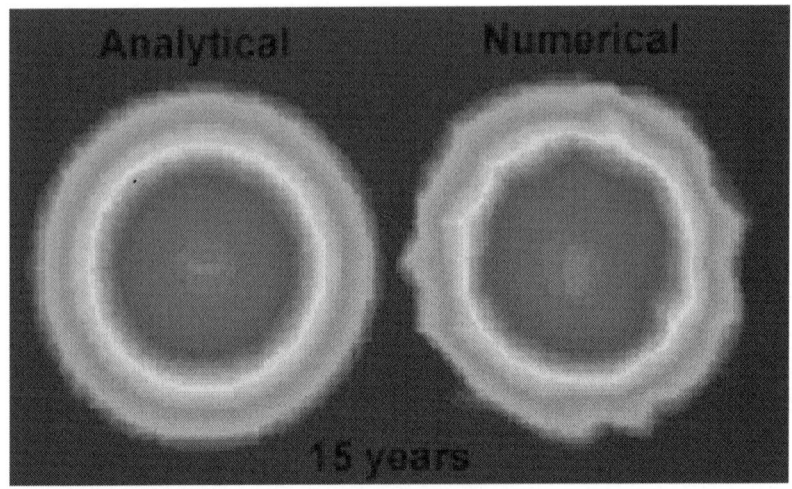

This next figure shows the results after 30 years simulation time:

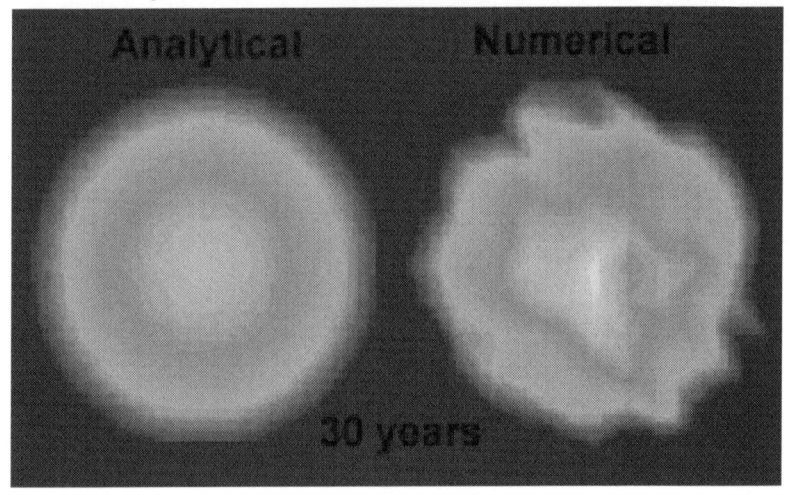

Dispersion is the next step in modeling complexity. It's basically diffusion driven by movement, thus dispersion is linked to the direction of flow, whereas diffusion is not. This next figure shows particle tracks without dispersion. The color indicates the age of the particles.

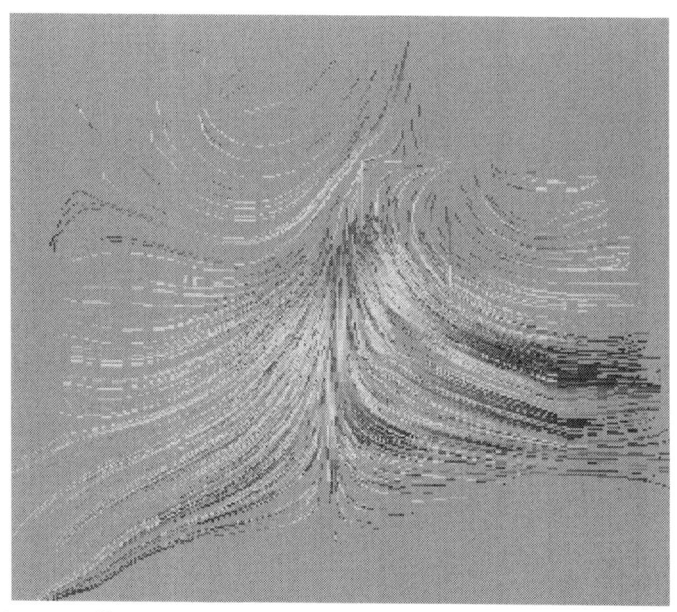

This next figure shows the particle track with dispersion (based on measured geological properties at the site):

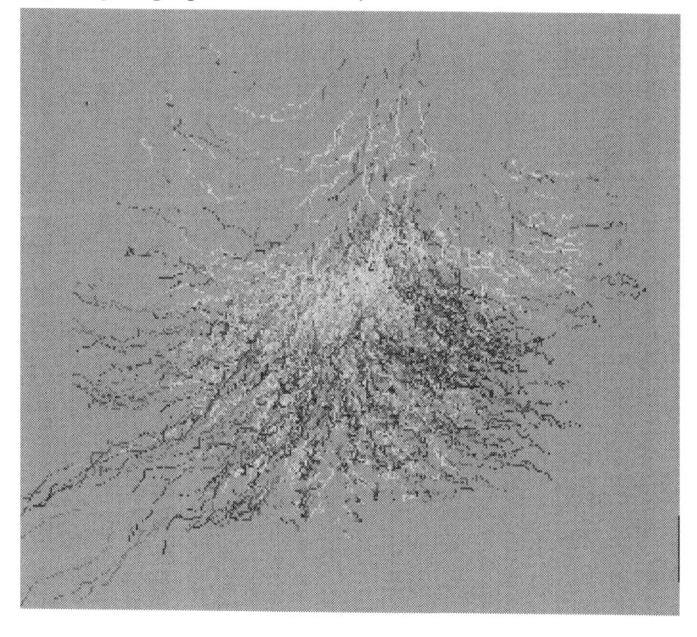

This same program can also handle fractured rock. Putting it all together creates an interesting pattern of the particles preferentially spreading through the ground like grout between tiles:

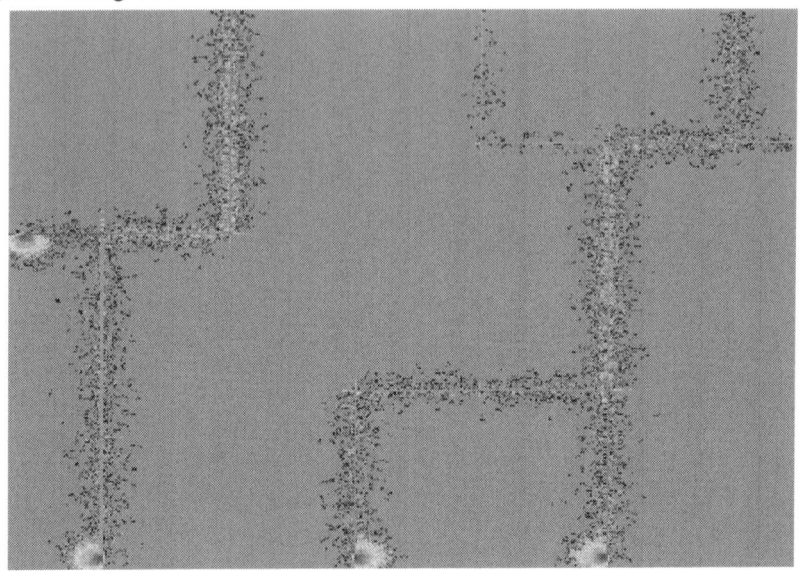

The advantage of this numerical solution that uses a random walk to simulate the behavior of transported contaminants is both geometry and properties. Complex three-dimensional geometry and varying properties preclude analytical solutions but are neatly solved numerically. This next figure illustrates the difference between diffusion and dispersion:

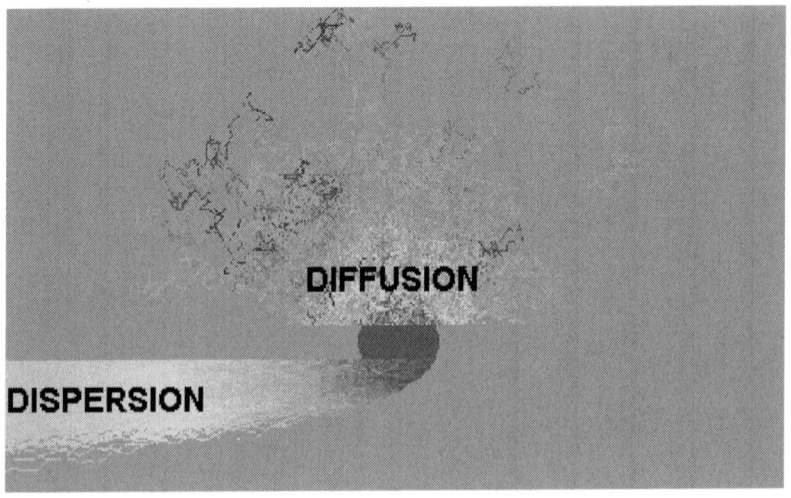

Chapter 12. Weather

Weather might seem random but it isn't. Not only does it exhibit complex—even mind-boggling—patterns, the parameters we use to measure weather (barometric pressure, temperature, humidity, wind speed and direction, and rainfall) are all interrelated. If you create random weather you will arrive at erroneous conclusions. There is no shortage of pseudo-scientific studies that have really messed up by going down this foolish path.

Years ago I was involved in a large study undertaken by the Federal Government of the United States to investigate the potential impacts of Global Warming on the nation's power supply system.[3] The power system simulation was my contribution to the overall effort. The team meteorologists generated the hypothetical weather by rearranging historical data.

The hottest, driest months on record don't all occur in the same year, neither do the coldest, wettest ones. The prevailing concept of Global Warming at the time was colder, wetter winters plus hotter, drier summers. The meteorologists took the three coldest, wettest months on record plus the three hottest, driest ones and put them into a single year to create a worst-case scenario. You never heard of the study because it didn't produce the desired outcome: The End of the World. No one tried to discredit the study because it had clearly been rigorous. Instead, they tried to bury and ignore it, an endeavor that was quite successful.

I have included a spreadsheet (temps42yr.xls) in the on-line archive that contains 42 years of hourly temperatures. These are from an airport located in a moderate climate. The coldest and hottest months are listed below by year:

extreme months	coldest		hottest	
	year	Tavg	year	Tavg
January	2003	27.2	1976	51.9
February	1984	32.3	1983	49.5
March	1986	36.7	1993	55.7
April	1987	52.2	1980	65.4
May	1987	62.1	1988	73.7
June	1987	70.0	1978	80.9
July	1993	70.9	2006	81.1
August	1993	71.8	2006	80.2
September	1993	64.6	1980	76.0
October	2013	52.4	2010	66.3
November	1976	41.9	2011	56.3
December	1989	30.2	1982	51.1

---

[3] Miller, B. A., V. Alavian, M. D. Bender, D. J. Benton, P. Ostrowski, Jr., H. M. Samples, and M. C. Shiao, "Sensitivity of the Tennessee Valley Authority Reservoir and Power Supply Systems to Changes in Meteorology," National Conference on Climate Change, 1992

The spreadsheet also contains three synthetic years: 1) all of the coldest months, 2) all of the hottest months, and 3) the coldest winter months plus the hottest summer months. The results are shown in this next figure:

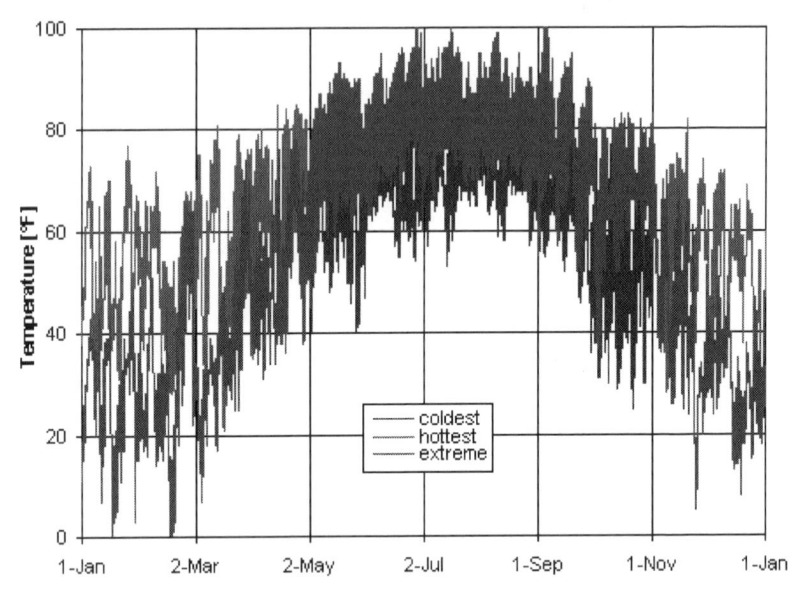

While these temperatures aren't random and so using them in a simulation isn't technically Monte Carlo, if you want meaningful results, this is the best way to do it. The same button creates data using months from random years:

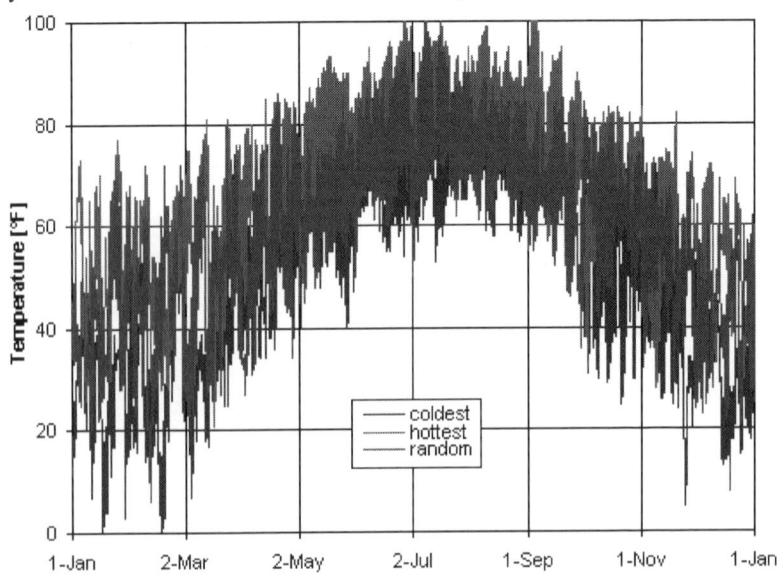

While randomly selecting months appears to work fairly well, keep in mind that weather parameters are related. If this were not so, you wouldn't see words like *fair* and *stormy* on a barometer. The following figures show the relationship between barometric pressure and temperature or relative humidity in one particular location:

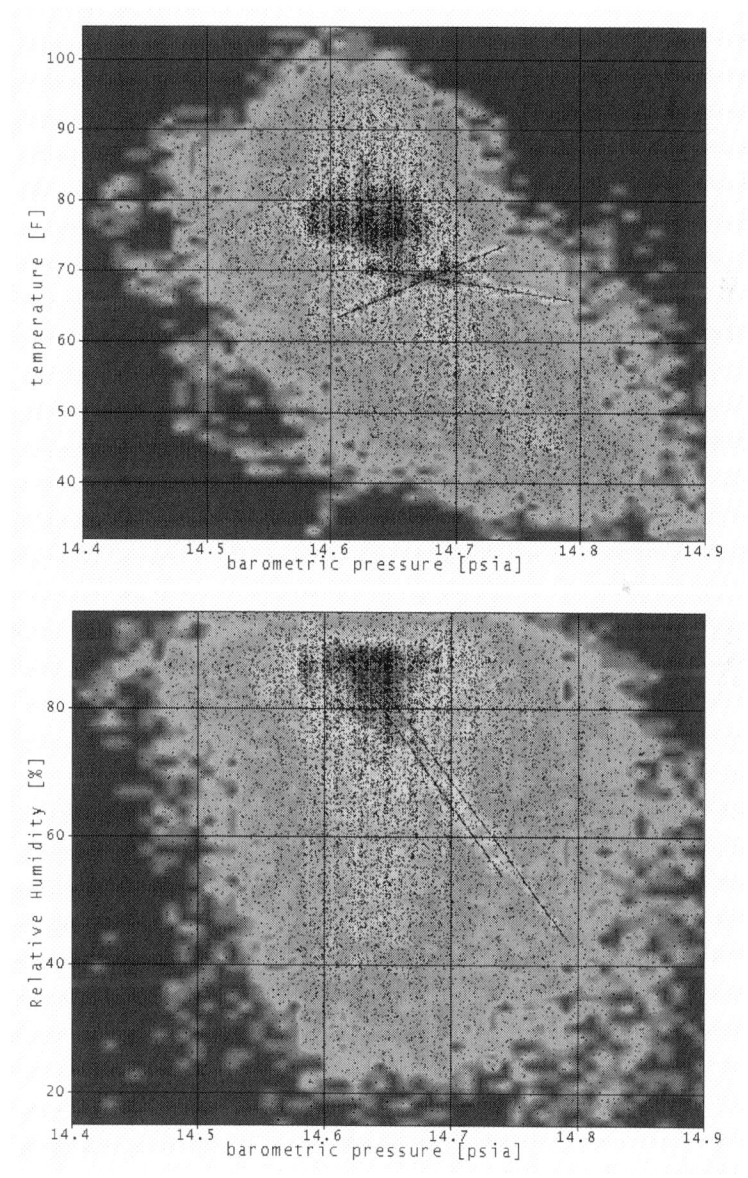

The black specks are data points. The gradation of colors (blue to green to yellow to orange to red) indicate the data density or how often the values occur in the combination indicated by the position on the graph. This next figure shows the relationship between temperature and relative humidity at this same location:

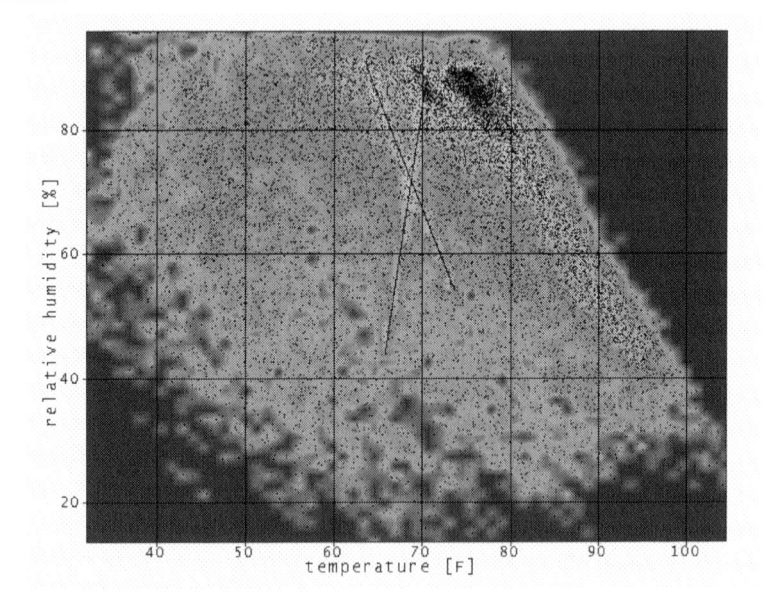

Chapter 13. Guessing

Locating minima or maxima and multi-dimensional integration are often given as examples of *sampling* within the context of Monte Carlo simulations. This process, however, is more like what we usually call *guessing*. Locating the lowest or highest elevation on a surface or estimating a complicated integral is used to illustrate this process of guessing. Neither one of these is particularly useful because: 1) by the time you've read in the surface topography you know where the minimum or maximum is and 2) Gauss Quadrature will always win out over guessing when it comes to any type of single- or multi-dimensional integration.[4]

Instead of these, we're going to consider a more useful application of guessing: *password cracking*. Prior to MSOffice®2007, Excel® used a 16-bit MD5 hash to encrypt passwords. Some MSO files still use this flimsy method. The following passwords are equivalent: abases, arises, azores, combos, cosmos, cubans, ingress, instep, selves, sifter, and sirras. So are: abated, Canada, curlew, eloper, excels, gauzes, omelet, repossessing, select, swords, unbreakability, and waives. Don't believe me? Try it for yourself and see.

I have provided a spreadsheet (passwords.xls) that's full of these synonyms plus a button to find even more. There are 49,811 passwords and 172,580 synonyms in this spreadsheet. You can paste in the entire unabridged dictionary if you like, push the button, and let 'er rip! In spite of the fact that there are many lengthy, complicated codes available on the Web, the MD5 algorithm shockingly simple to implement in C:

```
WORD MD5hash(BYTE*str,WORD len)
  {
  WORD l,w,v;
  for(w=l=0;l<len;l++)
    {
    v=str[l];
    v<<=l+1;
    w^=v;
    }
  w^=len;
  w^=0xCE4B;
  return(w);
  }
```

The source code (MD5.c) is also in the on-line archive along with a batch file to compile it. The hash result for the first list above (abases, arises, ...) is DB5F and for the second list (abated, Canada, ...) is DEEF. You can test the synonyms in Excel® by first protecting the workbook with one password and

---

[4] If you don't know how to use Gauss Quadrature for multi-dimensional integration, there's a ZIP file on my web site with code plus another one with a bunch of other integration methods.

then unprotecting it with one of the synonyms. You can pass each of these through the MD5 program, which will spit out the same hash for each list, proving beyond a shadow of a doubt that this *is* the algorithm used by Microsoft. This provides a meaningful, yet easy, way of comparing guessing strategies and timing how long it takes to crack the password using the same algorithm as MSO.[5]

We will first consider two password cracking algorithms and two variants of each. The first pair is a dictionary approach. I have provided a dictionary containing 191,215 words (see Appendix H, which also describes five more lists which could be used as passwords). The program to follow reads these in and then uses them as potential passwords. The first variant (methodical) simply tries each one sequentially until it finds a match. The second variant (gambler's luck) tries words randomly from the list, hoping to hit pick the right one sooner than later.

The second pair is a loop approach. It isn't a pure brute force loop approach. Believe me, I've tried it, and the brute force loop approach is orders of magnitude slower. This approach uses random loop bounds with a full loop only at the innermost level. This also has two variants: 1) a series of literal loops and 2) a loop of loops having a random depth.

I have selected the first 500 passwords to crack. I have also arbitrarily required each algorithm to achieve at least 95% success rate for these 500 words. Here is the code (crack.c):

```c
#define _CRT_SECURE_NO_DEPRECATE
#include <stdio.h>
#include <stdlib.h>
#include <string.h>
#include <malloc.h>
#define WIN32_LEAN_AND_MEAN
#include <windows.h>

size_t crack=500;

size_t lrand()
  {
  int i;
  union{BYTE b[4];size_t l;}u;
  for(i=0;i<sizeof(u);i++)
    u.b[i]=(BYTE)(rand()%256);
  return(u.l);
  }

WORD randbetween(WORD lo,WORD hi)
  {
```

---

[5] Too bad it's not bit coins, right? Perhaps in my next book...

```
    return(lo+rand()%(hi-lo+1));
    }

WORD MD5hash(BYTE*str,WORD len)
    {
    WORD l,w,v;
    for(w=l=0;l<len;l++)
        {
        v=str[l];
        v<<=l+1;
        w^=v;
        }
    w^=len;
    w^=0xCE4B;
    return(w);
    }

#define LONGEST 64

typedef struct{char txt[LONGEST+1];}WRD;

WRD*Wrd;
size_t nwrd=0;
size_t mwrd=10000;

size_t ReadWords(char*fname)
    {
    char bufr[LONGEST+2],*ptr;
    size_t l,m;
    FILE*fp;
    WRD*old;
    printf("reading words from: %s\n",fname);
    if((fp=fopen(fname,"rt"))==NULL)
        {
        printf("can't open file\n");
        exit(1);
        }
    if((Wrd=calloc(mwrd,sizeof(WRD)))==NULL)
        {
        printf("can't allocate memory\n");
        exit(1);
        }
    m=0;
    while(fgets(bufr,sizeof(bufr),fp))
        {
        l=strlen(bufr)-1;
        if(l<1)
            continue;
        if(l>m)
```

```c
      m=1;
    ptr=strchr(bufr,'\n');
    if(ptr==NULL)
      {
      printf("\nword on line %u is too long (>%u
    characters)\n%s\n",nwrd,(unsigned)LONGEST,bufr);
      exit(1);
      }
    *ptr=0;
    if(nwrd>=mwrd)
      {
      old=Wrd;
      mwrd+=10000;
      if((Wrd=calloc(mwrd,sizeof(WRD)))==NULL)
        {
        printf("can't allocate memory\n");
        exit(1);
        }
      memcpy(Wrd,old,nwrd*sizeof(WRD));
      free(old);
      }
    strcpy(Wrd[nwrd++].txt,bufr);
    }
  fclose(fp);
  printf("  %u words found, longest has %u
    characters\n",nwrd,m);
  return(nwrd);
  }

size_t DictionaryCrack1()
  {
  size_t fail,find,i,n;
  WORD hash;
  printf("using dictionary to crack %u
    passwords\n",min(crack,nwrd));
  printf("  employing a methodical approach\n");
  for(fail=find=n=0;n<min(nwrd,crack);n++)
    {
    hash=MD5hash(Wrd[n].txt,strlen(Wrd[n].txt));
    for(i=0;i<nwrd;i++)
      if(i!=n)
        if(MD5hash(Wrd[i].txt,strlen(Wrd[i].txt))==hash)
          break;
    if(i==nwrd)
      fail++;
    else
      find++;
    if((n+1)%100==0)
      printf("\r  %u of %u",n+1,min(crack,nwrd));
```

```
    }
  printf("\r    %u found and %u not found
    (%.1lf%%)\n",find,fail,find*100./(find+fail));
  return(find);
  }

size_t DictionaryCrack2()
  {
  size_t fail,find,i,l,n;
  WORD hash;
  printf("using dictionary to crack %u
    passwords\n",min(crack,nwrd));
  printf("   employing gambler's luck\n");
  for(fail=find=n=0;n<min(nwrd,crack);n++)
    {
    hash=MD5hash(Wrd[n].txt,strlen(Wrd[n].txt));
    for(l=0;l<nwrd/4;l++)
       {
       do{
         i=lrand()%nwrd;
         }while(i==n);
       if(MD5hash(Wrd[i].txt,strlen(Wrd[i].txt))==hash)
         goto found_it;
       }
    for(i=0;i<nwrd;i++)
       if(i!=n)
         if(MD5hash(Wrd[i].txt,strlen(Wrd[i].txt))==hash)
            goto found_it;
    fail++;
    goto next;
found_it:
    find++;
next:
    if((n+1)%100==0)
       printf("\r    %u of %u",n+1,min(crack,nwrd));
    }
  printf("\r    %u found and %u not found
    (%.1lf%%)\n",find,fail,find*100./(find+fail));
  return(find);
  }

size_t LoopCrack1()
  {
  BYTE pass[10];
  WORD
    hash,hi1,hi2,hi3,hi4,hi5,hi6,hi7,hi8,hi9,i1,i2,i3,i4,
    i5,i6,i7,i8,i9,i10,j,lo1,lo2,lo3,lo4,lo5,lo6,lo7,lo8,
    lo9;
  size_t fail,find,n;
```

```c
printf("using loops to crack %u
 passwords\n",min(crack,nwrd));
printf("  employing a methodical approach\n");
for(fail=find=n=0;n<min(nwrd,crack);n++)
  {
  hash=MD5hash(Wrd[n].txt,strlen(Wrd[n].txt));
  for(j=1;j<500;j++)
    {
    lo1=randbetween(97,121);
    lo2=randbetween(97,121);
    lo3=randbetween(97,121);
    lo4=randbetween(97,121);
    lo5=randbetween(97,121);
    lo6=randbetween(97,121);
    lo7=randbetween(97,121);
    lo8=randbetween(97,121);
    lo9=randbetween(97,121);
    hi1=lo1+1;
    hi2=lo2+1;
    hi3=lo3+1;
    hi4=lo4+1;
    hi5=lo5+1;
    hi6=lo6+1;
    hi7=lo7+1;
    hi8=lo8+1;
    hi9=lo9+1;
    memset(pass,0,sizeof(pass));
    for(i1=lo1;i1<hi1;i1++)
      {
      pass[0]=(BYTE)i1;
      if(MD5hash(pass,1)==hash)
        goto found_it;
      }
    for(i1=lo1;i1<hi1;i1++)
      {
      pass[0]=(BYTE)i1;
      for(i2=1;i2<255;i2++)
        {
        pass[1]=(BYTE)i2;
        if(MD5hash(pass,2)==hash)
          goto found_it;
        }
      }
    for(i1=lo1;i1<hi1;i1++)
      {
      pass[0]=(BYTE)i1;
      for(i2=lo2;i2<hi2;i2++)
        {
        pass[1]=(BYTE)i2;
```

```
      for(i3=1;i3<255;i3++)
         {
         pass[2]=(BYTE)i3;
         if(MD5hash(pass,3)==hash)
            goto found_it;
         }
      }
   }
for(i1=lo1;i1<hi1;i1++)
   {
   pass[0]=(BYTE)i1;
   for(i2=lo2;i2<hi2;i2++)
      {
      pass[1]=(BYTE)i2;
      for(i3=lo3;i3<hi3;i3++)
         {
         pass[2]=(BYTE)i3;
         for(i4=1;i4<255;i4++)
            {
            pass[3]=(BYTE)i4;
            if(MD5hash(pass,4)==hash)
               goto found_it;
            }
         }
      }
   }
for(i1=lo1;i1<hi1;i1++)
   {
   pass[0]=(BYTE)i1;
   for(i2=lo2;i2<hi2;i2++)
      {
      pass[1]=(BYTE)i2;
      for(i3=lo3;i3<hi3;i3++)
         {
         pass[2]=(BYTE)i3;
         for(i4=lo4;i4<hi4;i4++)
            {
            pass[3]=(BYTE)i4;
            for(i5=1;i5<255;i5++)
               {
               pass[4]=(BYTE)i5;
               if(MD5hash(pass,5)==hash)
                  goto found_it;
               }
            }
         }
      }
   }
for(i1=lo1;i1<hi1;i1++)
```

```
        {
        pass[0]=(BYTE)i1;
        for(i2=lo2;i2<hi2;i2++)
          {
          pass[1]=(BYTE)i2;
          for(i3=lo3;i3<hi3;i3++)
            {
            pass[2]=(BYTE)i3;
            for(i4=lo4;i4<hi4;i4++)
              {
              pass[3]=(BYTE)i4;
              for(i5=lo5;i5<hi5;i5++)
                {
                pass[4]=(BYTE)i5;
                for(i6=1;i6<255;i6++)
                  {
                  pass[5]=(BYTE)i6;
                  if(MD5hash(pass,6)==hash)
                    goto found_it;
                  }
                }
              }
            }
          }
        }
for(i1=lo1;i1<hi1;i1++)
  {
  pass[0]=(BYTE)i1;
  for(i2=lo2;i2<hi2;i2++)
    {
    pass[1]=(BYTE)i2;
    for(i3=lo3;i3<hi3;i3++)
      {
      pass[2]=(BYTE)i3;
      for(i4=lo4;i4<hi4;i4++)
        {
        pass[3]=(BYTE)i4;
        for(i5=lo5;i5<hi5;i5++)
          {
          pass[4]=(BYTE)i5;
          for(i6=lo6;i6<hi6;i6++)
            {
            pass[5]=(BYTE)i6;
            for(i7=1;i7<255;i7++)
              {
              pass[6]=(BYTE)i7;
              if(MD5hash(pass,7)==hash)
                goto found_it;
              }
```

```
                    }
                   }
                  }
                 }
                }
               }
      for(i1=lo1;i1<hi1;i1++)
        {
         pass[0]=(BYTE)i1;
         for(i2=lo2;i2<hi2;i2++)
            {
             pass[1]=(BYTE)i2;
             for(i3=lo3;i3<hi3;i3++)
                {
                 pass[2]=(BYTE)i3;
                 for(i4=lo4;i4<hi4;i4++)
                    {
                     pass[3]=(BYTE)i4;
                     for(i5=lo5;i5<hi5;i5++)
                        {
                         pass[4]=(BYTE)i5;
                         for(i6=lo6;i6<hi6;i6++)
                            {
                             pass[5]=(BYTE)i6;
                             for(i7=lo7;i7<hi7;i7++)
                                {
                                 pass[6]=(BYTE)i7;
                                 for(i8=1;i8<255;i8++)
                                    {
                                     pass[7]=(BYTE)i8;
                                     if(MD5hash(pass,8)==hash)
                                        goto found_it;
                                    }
                                }
                            }
                        }
                    }
                }
            }
        }
      for(i1=lo1;i1<hi1;i1++)
        {
         pass[0]=(BYTE)i1;
         for(i2=lo2;i2<hi2;i2++)
            {
             pass[1]=(BYTE)i2;
             for(i3=lo3;i3<hi3;i3++)
                {
                 pass[2]=(BYTE)i3;
```

```
            for(i4=lo4;i4<hi4;i4++)
               {
               pass[3]=(BYTE)i4;
               for(i5=lo5;i5<hi5;i5++)
                  {
                  pass[4]=(BYTE)i5;
                  for(i6=lo6;i6<hi6;i6++)
                     {
                     pass[5]=(BYTE)i6;
                     for(i7=lo7;i7<hi7;i7++)
                        {
                        pass[6]=(BYTE)i7;
                        for(i8=lo8;i8<hi8;i8++)
                           {
                           pass[7]=(BYTE)i8;
                           for(i9=1;i9<255;i9++)
                              {
                              pass[8]=(BYTE)i9;
                              if(MD5hash(pass,9)==hash)
                              goto found_it;
                              }
                           }
                        }
                     }
                  }
               }
            }
   for(i1=lo1;i1<hi1;i1++)
      {
      pass[0]=(BYTE)i1;
      for(i2=lo2;i2<hi2;i2++)
         {
         pass[1]=(BYTE)i2;
         for(i3=lo3;i3<hi3;i3++)
            {
            pass[2]=(BYTE)i3;
            for(i4=lo4;i4<hi4;i4++)
               {
               pass[3]=(BYTE)i4;
               for(i5=lo5;i5<hi5;i5++)
                  {
                  pass[4]=(BYTE)i5;
                  for(i6=lo6;i6<hi6;i6++)
                     {
                     pass[5]=(BYTE)i6;
                     for(i7=lo7;i7<hi7;i7++)
                        {
```

```
                    pass[6]=(BYTE)i7;
                    for(i8=lo8;i8<hi8;i8++)
                      {
                      pass[7]=(BYTE)i8;
                      for(i9=lo9;i9<hi9;i9++)
                        {
                        pass[8]=(BYTE)i9;
                        for(i10=1;i10<255;i10++)
                          {
                          pass[9]=(BYTE)i10;
                          if(MD5hash(pass,10)==hash)
                            goto found_it;
                          }
                        }
                      }
                    }
                  }
                }
              }
            }
          }
        }
      }
    }
    fail++;
    goto next;
found_it:
    find++;
next:
    if((n+1)%100==0)
      printf("\r   %u of %u",n+1,min(crack,nwrd));
    }
  printf("\r   %u found and %u not found
    (%.1lf%%)\n",find,fail,find*100./(find+fail));
  return(find);
  }

size_t LoopCrack2()
  {
  BYTE pass[16];
  WORD hash;
  size_t fail,find,i,l,m,n;
  printf("using loops to crack %u
    passwords\n",min(crack,nwrd));
  printf("  employing gambler's luck\n");
  for(fail=find=n=0;n<min(nwrd,crack);n++)
    {
    hash=MD5hash(Wrd[n].txt,strlen(Wrd[n].txt));
    for(i=1;i<300000;i++)
      {
```

65

```
      m=1+(rand()%(sizeof(pass)-1));
      for(l=0;l<m;l++)
        pass[l]=(BYTE)(rand()%255);
      if(MD5hash(pass,m)==hash)
        goto found_it;
      }
    fail++;
    goto next;
found_it:
    find++;
next:
    if((n+1)%100==0)
      printf("\r   %u of %u",n+1,min(crack,nwrd));
    }
  printf("\r   %u found and %u not found
    (%.1lf%%)\n",find,fail,find*100./(find+fail));
  return(find);
}

int main(int argc,char**argv,char**envp)
{
  size_t n;
  DWORD t0,t1,t2;

  t0=t1=GetTickCount();
  printf("comparing password cracking algorithms\n");

  n=ReadWords("words.txt");
  t2=GetTickCount();
  printf("  elapsed time: %.3lf seconds\n",(t2-
    t1)/1000.);
  t1=t2;

  n=DictionaryCrack1();
  t2=GetTickCount();
  printf("  elapsed time: %.3lf seconds (%.0lf
    words/sec)\n",(t2-t1)/1000.,n/((t2-t1)/1000.));
  t1=t2;

  n=DictionaryCrack2();
  t2=GetTickCount();
  printf("  elapsed time: %.3lf seconds (%.0lf
    words/sec)\n",(t2-t1)/1000.,n/((t2-t1)/1000.));
  t1=t2;

  n=LoopCrack1();
  t2=GetTickCount();
  printf("  elapsed time: %.3lf seconds (%.0lf
    words/sec)\n",(t2-t1)/1000.,n/((t2-t1)/1000.));
```

```
        t1=t2;

        n=LoopCrack2();
        t2=GetTickCount();
        printf("   elapsed time: %.3lf seconds (%.01f
          words/sec)\n",(t2-t1)/1000.,n/((t2-t1)/1000.));
        t1=t2;

        t2=GetTickCount();
        printf("total elapsed time: %.3lf seconds\n",(t2-
          t0)/1000.);

        return(0);
        }
```

Here is the output:

```
comparing password cracking algorithms
reading words from: words.txt
   191215 words found, longest has 45 characters
   elapsed time: 0.297 seconds
using dictionary to crack 500 passwords
   employing a methodical approach
   480 found and 20 not found (96.0%)
   elapsed time: 0.531 seconds (904 words/sec)
using dictionary to crack 500 passwords
   employing gambler's luck
   480 found and 20 not found (96.0%)
   elapsed time: 2.735 seconds (176 words/sec)
using loops to crack 500 passwords
   employing a methodical approach
   487 found and 13 not found (97.4%)
   elapsed time: 1.296 seconds (376 words/sec)
using loops to crack 500 passwords
   employing gambler's luck
   475 found and 25 not found (95.0%)
   elapsed time: 14.579 seconds (33 words/sec)
total elapsed time: 19.438 seconds
```

I takes only 0.297 second to read in all 191,215 words. The methodical variant of the dictionary approach is 96.0% successful and cracks on average 904 passwords per second. The gambler's luck variant is equally effective, but only cracks 176 passwords per second. The methodical variant of the loop approach is 97.4% successful and cracks 376 passwords per second. The gambler's luck variant of the loop method is 95% successful and cracks only 33 passwords per second.

While this isn't an exhaustive test of all algorithms or all encryption schemes, it does illustrate two things that are fairly general: 1) the dictionary approach works better than the loop approach and 2) the methodical approach works better than the gambler's luck.

Appendix A: Random Number Generation

The rand() function in C returns uniformly-distributed random numbers between 0 and 32767, that is 15-bit unsigned integers. These are only approximately distributed uniformly, but in most cases this is adequate. The algorithm used to generate these numbers in the ANSI standard library is:

```
static unsigned long int next=1;
short int rand(void)
  {
  next=next*1103515245UL+12345UL;
  return((unsigned short int)(next/0x10000UL)&0x7FFF);
  }
```

This algorithm relies on repetitive multiplication resulting in an overflow condition each time and is typical. The standard numeric library has another function that is sometimes used which is:

```
short int random(short int num)
  {
  next=next*1103515245UL+12345UL;
  return(((next/0x10000UL)*(unsigned)num)>>16);
  }
```

The sequence of random numbers always starts at the same place unless it is seeded. The two seeding functions in the standard library are:

```
void srand(unsigned short int seed)
  {
  next=seed;
  }
void randomize(void)
  {
  next=(unsigned long)time(NULL);
  }
```

Excel® has a function, RAND(), which returns a random real number between zero and one. This is just equal to rand()/32767. The VBA® (i.e., macro) equivalent is Rnd(). Should you require a signed random number, it is simple enough to adapt the previous function as follows:

```
signed short int irand()
  {
  i=rand();
  if(rand()&1)
    return(-i);
  return(i);
  }
```

There are many more complicated algorithms for generating random numbers that can readily be found on the Internet. These are primarily of academic interest and only minimal practical value. Should you need 31-bit (or larger) random numbers, these can easily be generated as follows:

```
DWORD drand()
  {
  union{DWORD d;BYTE b[4];}u;
  u.b[0]=(BYTE)(rand()&0xFF);
  u.b[1]=(BYTE)(rand()&0xFF);
  u.b[2]=(BYTE)(rand()&0xFF);
  u.b[3]=(BYTE)(rand()&0x7F);
  return(u.d);
  }
```

These are uniformly-distributed random numbers, that is, random numbers that have a flat probability distribution. What we most often need is normally distributed random numbers that have a bell-shaped probability distribution. The simplest way to produce normally distributed integers from uniformly-distributed ones is the following formula:

```
int nrand()
  {
  int i,r;
  for(r=i=0;i<12;i++)
    r+=rand();
  return(r/12);
  }
```

A slight modification of this formula can be used to create normally-distributed real numbers having a mean of 0 and a standard deviation of 1:

```
double randnorm()
  {
  int i;
  double r;
  for(r=i=0;i<12;i++)
    r+=rand()/32767.;
  return((r-6.)/6.);
  }
```

The function above can be used to create normally-distributed numbers having a mean of *a* and s standard deviation of *s*:

```
double randist(double a,double s)
  {
  return(a+6.*s*randnorm());
  }
```

While there have been many papers written on the deficiencies of various random number generating algorithms, such as the one used in rand(), these are rarely the weak links in a Monte Carlo simulation. There are five basic tests of randomness:

1) the frequency test (some numbers should not appear much more or less often than other number),
2) the runs test (no patterns where sequential numbers run up or down like a saw tooth),

3) the autocorrelation test (repeating sequences),
4) the gap test (if you test enough random numbers you should eventually get all of the ones within the expected range, that is, no gaps or missing numbers), and
5) the poker test (frequency with which digits are repeated within a single number).

One way of visualizing the frequency and gap tests is by plotting specks inside a circle. This figure uses Excel's RAND() function to generate X and Y coordinates, then $R=SQRT(X^2+Y^2)$, and finally plotting all the points with R<1 in one color and R>1 in another:

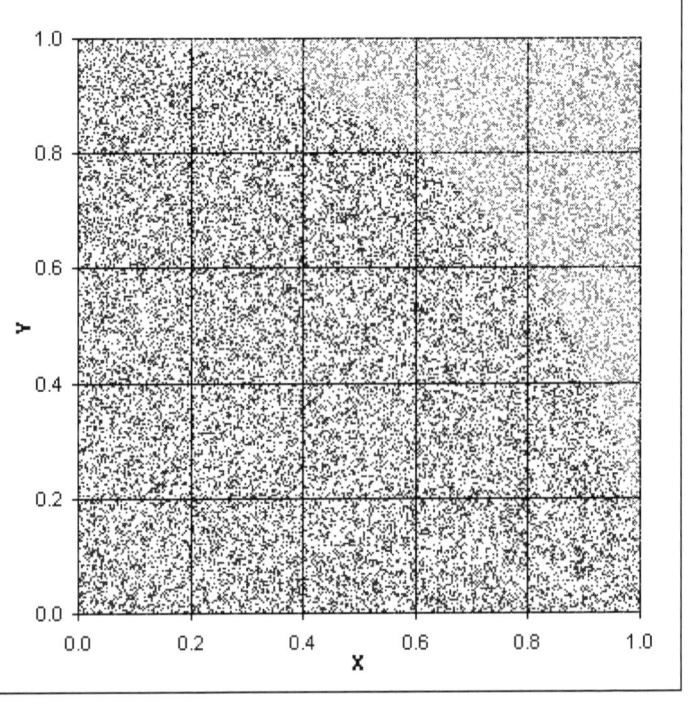

Zooming in to 400% reveals the clumpiness:

This is a result of the sampling, not a failure of the algorithm. Expanding the number of points to 256*1024 fills in all of these gaps:

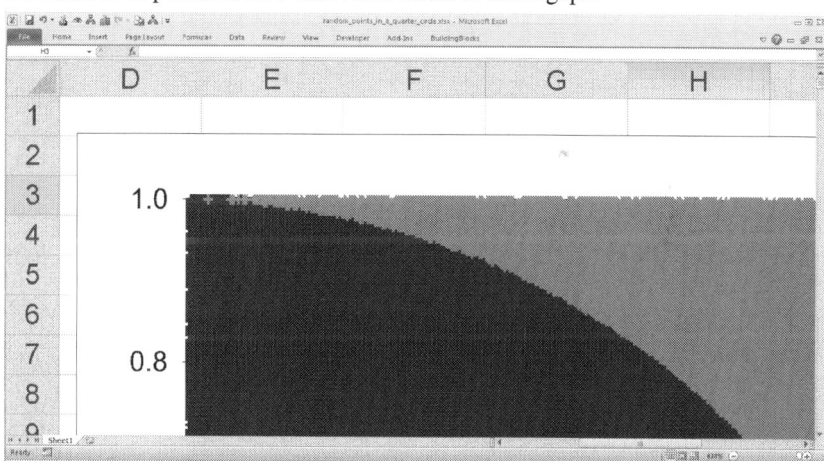

The following program demonstrates the lack of gaps in the ANSI standard library function:

```
#include <stdio.h>
#include <stdlib.h>
int count[32768];
int main(int argc,char**argv,char**envp)
  {
  int i,j;
  for(i=0;i<32768*16;i++)
    count[rand()]++;
```

```
    for(i=j=0;i<32768;i++)
      if(count[i]==0)
        printf("%i ",i,j++);
    printf("\ngaps=%i\n",j);
    return(0);
    }
gaps=0
```

You also may need to generate discrete random integers. In Excel® you can use RANDBETWEEN(lo,hi) to return an integer and the values may exceed 32767, but don't presume that the granularity of this function exceeds 15-bit. These will be uniformly-distributed. It is rare that you would ever need to generate normally-distributed discrete integers. The following code is equivalent to Excel's RANDBETWEEN()

```
int randbetween(int lo,int hi)
{
return lo+rand()%(hi-lo+1);
}
```

Appendix B. Two-Way & Three-Way Gunfight

The following code implements both a two-way and three-way gunfight.

```c
#include <stdio.h>
#include <stdlib.h>
#include <time.h>

typedef struct{
  char*name;
  double accuracy,speed,lucky; /* attributes */
  int alive,lethal,quick,luck; /* conditions */
  }gunslinger;

gunslinger g1={"Blondie"  ,0.75,0.75,0.75,0,0,0,0};
   /* fast, accurate, & lucky */
gunslinger g2={"AngelEyes",0.50,0.50,0.50,0,0,0,0};
   /* all round average */
gunslinger g3={"Tuco"     ,0.50,0.75,0.25,0,0,0,0};
   /* fast but unlucky */

void Draw(gunslinger*man)
  {/* randomly set speed, lethality, and luck based on
    attributes */
  if(man->alive)
    {
    man->quick=(int)(man->speed*rand());
    man->lethal=((man->accuracy*32767)>=rand());
    man->luck  =((man->lucky   *32767)>=rand());
    }
  else
    man->quick=man->lethal=man->luck=0;
  }

void sort(gunslinger**guns,int n)
  {/* bubble sort on draw: fast to slow */
  int i,j;
  gunslinger*g;
  do{
    for(j=i=0;i<n-1;i++)
      {
      if(guns[i]->quick<guns[i+1]->quick)
        {
        g=guns[i];
        guns[i]=guns[i+1];
        guns[i+1]=g;
        j=1;
        }
      }
    }while(j);
```

```c
  }

int TwoDraw(gunslinger*man1,gunslinger*man2)
  {
  gunslinger*draw[2];
  Draw(man1);
  Draw(man2);
  draw[0]=man1;
  draw[1]=man2;
  sort(draw,2);
  if(draw[0]->lethal)
    draw[1]->alive=0; /* g1 kills g2 */
  else if(draw[1]->lethal)
    draw[0]->alive=0; /* g2 kills g1 */
  return(man1->alive&&man2->alive);
  }

void TwoWay(gunslinger*man1,gunslinger*man2)
  {
  int shot=0;
  man1->alive=man2->alive=1;
  printf("%-9s vs. %-9s",man1->name,man2->name);
  do{shot++;
    }while(TwoDraw(man1,man2));
  printf(" survivor: %-9s after %i shot%s\n",man1-
    >alive?man1->name:man2->name,shot,shot>1?"s":"");
  }

int ThreeDraw(gunslinger*man1,gunslinger*man2,
gunslinger*man3)
  {
  gunslinger*draw[3];
  Draw(man1);
  Draw(man2);
  Draw(man3);
  draw[0]=man1;
  draw[1]=man2;
  draw[2]=man3;
  sort(draw,3);
  if(!draw[2]->alive) /* g2 is already dead */
    return(TwoDraw(draw[0],draw[1]));
  if(draw[0]->lethal)
    {
    if(draw[0]->luck)
      draw[1]->alive=0; /* g1 kills g2 */
    else
      draw[2]->alive=0; /* g1 kills g3 */
    }
  if(draw[1]->alive) /* if g2 is still alive */
```

```c
      {
      if(draw[1]->lethal)
        {
        if(draw[1]->luck)
          draw[0]->alive=0; /* g2 kills g1 */
        else
          draw[2]->alive=0; /* g2 kills g3 */
        }
      }
    if(draw[2]->alive) /* if g3 is still alive */
      {
      if(draw[2]->lethal)
        {
        if(draw[2]->luck)
          draw[0]->alive=0; /* g3 kills g1 */
        else
          draw[1]->alive=0; /* g3 kills g1 */
        }
      }
    return((man1->alive&&man2->alive)||
           (man1->alive&&man3->alive)||
           (man2->alive&&man3->alive));
    }

void
  ThreeWay(gunslinger*man1,gunslinger*man2,gunslinger*m
  an3)
  {
  int shot=0;
  man1->alive=man2->alive=man3->alive=1;
  printf("%s vs. %s vs. %s",man1->name,man2->name,man3-
    >name);
  do{shot++;
    }while(ThreeDraw(man1,man2,man3));
  printf(" survivor: %-9s after %i shot%s\n",man1-
    >alive?man1->name:man2->alive?man2->name:man3-
    >name,shot,shot>1?"s":"");
  }

int main(int argc,char**argv,char**envp)
  {
  int duel;
  time_t t;
  time(&t);
  srand((unsigned)t);
  for(duel=1;duel<=5;duel++)
    TwoWay(&g1,&g2);
  for(duel=1;duel<=5;duel++)
    TwoWay(&g1,&g3);
```

```
for(duel=1;duel<=5;duel++)
  TwoWay(&g2,&g3);
for(duel=1;duel<=5;duel++)
  ThreeWay(&g1,&g2,&g3);
return(0);
}
```

Appendix C. Slot Machine Code
The following code simulates the slot machine described in Chapter 3.

```c
#include <stdio.h>
#include <stdlib.h>

char*picts[6]={"bar","cherry","plum","bell","orange",
"lemon"};
int reel1[21]={0,1,4,3,2,0,1,5,3,2,4,5,3,2,4,1,5,0,
4,3,5};
int reel2[21]={0,2,3,4,5,0,1,2,3,4,5,1,2,3,4,5,2,3,
4,5,1};
int reel3[21]={0,4,5,3,2,4,1,3,5,4,2,5,1,4,5,3,4,5,
3,2,5};

int payout(int r1,int r2,int r3)
  {
  if(r1==0&&r2==0&&r3==0)
    return(170);
  if(r1==1&&r2==1&&r3==1)
    return(56);
  if(r1==2&&r2==2&&r3==2)
    return(28);
  if(r1==3&&r2==3&&r3==3)
    return(16);
  if(r1==4&&r2==4&&r3==4)
    return(12);
  if(r1==5&&r2==5&&r3==5)
    return(10);
 if((r1==0&&r2==0)||(r1==0&&r3==0)||(r2==0&&r3==0))
    return(4);
 if((r1==1&&r2==1)||(r1==1&&r3==1)||(r2==1&&r3==1))
    return(2);
 if((r1==2&&r2==2)||(r1==2&&r3==2)||(r2==2&&r3==2))
    return(1);
  return(0);
  }

int main(int argc,char**argv,char**envp)
  {
  int i,p,r1,r2,r3,s;
  for(s=0,i=1;i<1000000;i++)
    {
    r1=reel1[rand()%21];
    r2=reel2[rand()%21];
    r3=reel3[rand()%21];
    p=payout(r1,r2,r3);
    s+=p;
    if(p>10)
```

```
      printf("%6i %i %i %i %3i
 %lf\n",i,r1,r2,r3,p,s/((double)i));
   }
 return(0);
 }
```

Appendix D. Slot Machine Code

The following code randomly sorts the pictures on the reels of the slot machine described in Chapter 3 to arrive at a best order.

```
#include <stdio.h>
#include <stdlib.h>
#include <string.h>

char*picts[6]={"bar","cherry","plum","bell","orange",
   "lemon"};

char*reel1[21]={"bar","cherry","plum","bell","orange",
   "lemon","bar","cherry","plum","bell","orange",
   "lemon","bar","cherry","plum","bell","orange","lemon",
   "bell","orange","lemon"};

char*reel2[21]={"bar","plum","bell","orange","lemon",
   "bar","cherry","plum","bell","orange","lemon",
   "cherry","plum","bell","orange","lemon","plum",
   "bell","orange","lemon","cherry"};

char*reel3[21]={"bar","orange","lemon","cherry","plum",
   "bell","orange","lemon","plum","bell","orange",
   "lemon","bell","orange","lemon","orange","lemon",
   "lemon","cherry","plum","bell"};

int score(char**reel,char*pict)
   {
   int i,j,k,l;
   for(l=21,i=0;i<21;i++)
      {
      if(strcmp(reel[i],pict)==0)
         {
         for(j=1;j<21;j++)
            {
            k=(i+j)%21;
            if(strcmp(reel[k],pict)==0)
               l=min(l,abs(k-i));
            }
         }
      }
   return(l);
   }

int Score(char**reel)
   {
   int i,l;
   for(l=21,i=0;i<6;i++)
      l=min(l,score(reel,picts[i]));
```

79

```
      return(l);
      }

void ShuffleList(int*list)
    {
    int i,j,k,l;;
    for(i=0;i<256;i++)
        {
        j=rand()%19;
        k=rand()%19;
        if(j!=k)
            {
            l=list[j];
            list[j]=list[k];
            list[k]=l;
            }
        }
    }

void ShuffleReel(char**reel)
    {
    char*rold[19];
    int i,list[19];
    for(i=0;i<19;i++)
        {
        list[i]=i;
        rold[i]=reel[i+2];
        }
    ShuffleList(list);
    for(i=0;i<19;i++)
        reel[i+2]=rold[list[i]];
    }

void OptimizeReel(char**reel)
    {
    char*best[21];
    int i,j,k,l;
    j=Score(reel);
    if(j>3)
        return;
    memcpy(best,reel,sizeof(best));
    for(i=0;i<65536;i++)
        {
        ShuffleReel(reel);
        k=Score(reel);
        if(k<=j)
            continue;
        for(l=0;l<21;l++)
            printf("%s ",reel[l]);
```

```c
      printf("%i\n",k);
      memcpy(best,reel,sizeof(best));
      j=k;
      if(j>3)
        break;
    }
  memcpy(reel,best,sizeof(best));
  }

int main(int argc,char**argv,char**envp)
  {
  int i;
  for(i=0;i<21;i++)
    printf("%-6s %-6s %-
    6s\n",reel1[i],reel2[i],reel3[i]);
  printf("%-6i %-6i %-
    6i\n",Score(reel1),Score(reel2),Score(reel3));
  OptimizeReel(reel1);
  OptimizeReel(reel2);
  OptimizeReel(reel3);
  for(i=0;i<21;i++)
    printf("%-6s %-6s %-
    6s\n",reel1[i],reel2[i],reel3[i]);
  printf("%-6i %-6i %-
    6i\n",Score(reel1),Score(reel2),Score(reel3));
  return(0);
  }
```

Appendix E. Card Deck Shuffling Program

The following program simulates shuffling a deck of cards:

```
#define _CRT_SECURE_NO_DEPRECATE
#include <stdio.h>
#include <stdlib.h>
#include <string.h>
#include <time.h>

typedef struct{int f,s;}card;
typedef struct{card c[52];}deck;

void initialize(deck*d)
  {
  short f,i,s;
  printf("initializing deck\n");
  for(i=s=0;s<4;s++)
    {
    for(f=0;f<13;f++,i++)
      {
      d->c[i].f=f;
      d->c[i].s=s;
      }
    }
  }

double score(deck*d)
  {
  int f,i,j,k,l;
  double s=0.;
  for(i=0;i<51+52;)  /* increasing straights */
    {
    for(f=l=1;i+l<52;l++)
      {
      j=(i+l)%52;
      k=(i+l-1)%52;
      if(d->c[j].f!=d->c[k].f+1)
        break;
      else if(d->c[j].s!=d->c[k].s)
        f=0;
      }
    if(f&&l>1)   /* straight flush */
      s+=pow(13,l-1)*pow(4,l-1);
    else if(l>1)
      s+=pow(13,l-1);
    i+=l;
    }
  for(i=0;i<51+52;)  /* decreasing straights */
    {
```

82

```
      for(f=l=1;i+l<52;l++)
        {
        j=(i+l)%52;
        k=(i+l-1)%52;
        if(d->c[j].f!=d->c[k].f-1)
          break;
        else if(d->c[j].s!=d->c[k].s)
          f=0;
        }
      if(f&&l>1) /* straight flush */
        s+=pow(13,l-1)*pow(4,l-1);
      else if(l>1)
        s+=pow(13,l-1);
      i+=l;
      }
    for(i=0;i<51+52;)  /* 2, 3, 4 of a kind */
      {
      for(l=1;i+l<52;l++)
        {
        j=(i+l)%52;
        k=(i+l-1)%52;
        if(d->c[j].f!=d->c[k].f)
          break;
        }
      if(l>1)
        s+=pow(4,l-1);
      i+=l;
      }
    return s;
    }

void shuffle(deck*d,int n)
  {
  int i,j,k;
  card c;
  if(n>1)
    printf("shuffling deck (%i swaps)\n",n);
  for(i=0;i<n;i++)
    {
    do{
      j=rand()%52;
      k=rand()%52;
      }while(k==j);
    c=d->c[j];
    d->c[j]=d->c[k];
    d->c[k]=c;
    }
  }
```

```
char*face[13]={"A","2","3","4","5","6","7","8","9","10",
   "J","Q","K"};
char*suit[4]={"S","H","D","C"};

void list(deck*d,int show)
  {
  char ccc[]="???";
  int i;
  if(show)
     {
     for(i=0;i<52;i++)
        {
        strcpy(ccc,face[d->c[i].f]);
        strcat(ccc,suit[d->c[i].s]);
        if((i+1)%13)
           printf("%-3s ",ccc);
        else
           printf("%s\n",ccc);
        }
     }
  printf("score=%.0lf\n",score(d));
  }

int main(int argc,char**argv,char**envp)
  {
  int i;
  deck d;
  time_t t;
  time(&t);
  srand((unsigned int)t);
  initialize(&d);
  list(&d,0);
  for(i=1;i<52;i++)
     {
     shuffle(&d,1);
     list(&d,0);
     }
  return(0);
  }
```

Appendix F. Systematic Bias Program

The following program produces a distribution having no bias, uncorrelated bias, and correlated bias. This simulation uses heat exchanger performance calculations as the basis for illustration.

```
#define _CRT_SECURE_NO_DEPRECATE
#include <stdio.h>
#include <stddef.h>
#include <stdlib.h>
#include <string.h>
#include <malloc.h>
#define _USE_MATH_DEFINES
#include <float.h>
#include <math.h>

double rdist(double mean,double stdev)
  {
  int i,s;
  for(s=i=0;i<12;i++)
    s+=rand();
  return(mean+stdev*(s/32767.-6.));
  }

double Cp(double T)
  {
  double x;
  x=T/1000.;
  return((((86.1141955*x-43.463356)*x+8.81131308)*x-
    0.805905686)*x+1.02536581);
  }

double LMTD(double dT1,double dT2)
  {
  if(dT1<=0.)
    return(0.);
  if(dT2<=0.)
    return(0.);
  if(fabs(dT1-dT2)<0.0001)
    return(sqrt(dT1*dT2));
  return((dT1-dT2)/log(dT1/dT2));
  }

int CompareDoubles(const void*v1,const void*v2)
  {
  double u1,u2;
  u1=*(double*)v1;
  u2=*(double*)v2;
  if(u1>u2)
    return(1);
```

```c
      if(u1<u2)
        return(-1);
      return(0);
      }

    #define bins (51*2)
    #define cases (10*1000*1000)

    struct{double bias;}CP={0.0005};
    struct{double avg,bias,stdev;}
      FH ={ 6.00,0.005,0.0058},
      FC ={10.22,0.005,0.0067},
      THI={95.27,0.5,0.125},
      THO={85.53,0.5,0.137},
      TCI={79.91,0.5,0.135},
      TCO={85.75,0.5,0.127},
      AREA={0.01873,0.001,0.};

    FILE*fp;

    void Calculate(int bias,int correlated)
      {
      int*bin,i,j;
      double area,Cc,Ch,Fc,Fh,Qa,Qc,Qh,Tci,Tco,Thi,Tho;
      double U,U95,*Ui,Umax,Umean,Umedian,Umin;

      printf("calculating\n");
      fprintf(fp,"bias=%s,
        correlated=%s\n",bias?"T":"F",correlated?"T":"F");

      Ui=calloc(cases,sizeof(double));
      bin=calloc(bins,sizeof(int));

      for(Umean=i=0;i<cases;i++)
        {
        area=AREA.avg;
        if(bias&&correlated)
          {
          if(rand()%2)
            area=AREA.avg*(1.+AREA.bias);
          else
            area=AREA.avg*(1.-AREA.bias);
          if(rand()%2)
            {
            Fh=FH.avg*rdist(1.,FH.stdev)*(1.+FH.bias);
            Fc=FC.avg*rdist(1.,FC.stdev)*(1.+FC.bias);
            }
          else
            {
```

```
    Fh=FH.avg*rdist(1.,FH.stdev)*(1.+FH.bias);
    Fc=FC.avg*rdist(1.,FC.stdev)*(1.-FC.bias);
    }
  if(rand()%2)
    {
    Thi=rdist(THI.avg,THI.stdev)+THI.bias;
    Tho=rdist(THO.avg,THO.stdev)+THO.bias;
    Tci=rdist(TCI.avg,TCI.stdev)+TCI.bias;
    Tco=rdist(TCO.avg,TCO.stdev)+TCI.bias;
    }
  else
    {
    Thi=rdist(THI.avg,THI.stdev)-THI.bias;
    Tho=rdist(THO.avg,THO.stdev)-THO.bias;
    Tci=rdist(TCI.avg,TCI.stdev)-TCI.bias;
    Tco=rdist(TCO.avg,TCO.stdev)-TCI.bias;
    }
  if(rand()%2)
    Ch=Cp((Thi+Tho)/2.)*(1.+CP.bias);
  else
    Ch=Cp((Thi+Tho)/2.)*(1.-CP.bias);
  if(rand()%2)
    Cc=Cp((Tci+Tco)/2.)*(1.+CP.bias);
  else
    Cc=Cp((Tci+Tco)/2.)*(1.+CP.bias);
  }
else if(bias)
  {
  if(rand()%2)
    area=AREA.avg*(1.+AREA.bias);
  else
    area=AREA.avg*(1.-AREA.bias);
  if(rand()%2)
    Fh=FH.avg*rdist(1.,FH.stdev)*(1.+FH.bias);
  else
    Fh=FH.avg*rdist(1.,FH.stdev)*(1.+FH.bias);
  if(rand()%2)
    Fc=FC.avg*rdist(1.,FC.stdev)*(1.+FC.bias);
  else
    Fc=FC.avg*rdist(1.,FC.stdev)*(1.-FC.bias);
  if(rand()%2)
    Thi=rdist(THI.avg,THI.stdev)+THI.bias;
  else
    Thi=rdist(THI.avg,THI.stdev)-THI.bias;
  if(rand()%2)
    Tho=rdist(THO.avg,THO.stdev)+THO.bias;
  else
    Tho=rdist(THO.avg,THO.stdev)-THO.bias;
  if(rand()%2)
```

```
            Tci=rdist(TCI.avg,TCI.stdev)+TCI.bias;
        else
            Tci=rdist(TCI.avg,TCI.stdev)-TCI.bias;
        if(rand()%2)
            Tco=rdist(TCO.avg,TCO.stdev)+TCI.bias;
        else
            Tco=rdist(TCO.avg,TCO.stdev)-TCI.bias;
        if(rand()%2)
            Ch=Cp((Thi+Tho)/2.)*(1.+CP.bias);
        else
            Ch=Cp((Thi+Tho)/2.)*(1.-CP.bias);
        if(rand()%2)
            Cc=Cp((Tci+Tco)/2.)*(1.+CP.bias);
        else
            Cc=Cp((Tci+Tco)/2.)*(1.+CP.bias);
        }
    else
        {
        Fh=FH.avg*rdist(1.,FH.stdev);
        Fc=FC.avg*rdist(1.,FC.stdev);
        Thi=rdist(THI.avg,THI.stdev);
        Tho=rdist(THO.avg,THO.stdev);
        Tci=rdist(TCI.avg,TCI.stdev);
        Tco=rdist(TCO.avg,TCO.stdev);
        Ch=Cp((Thi+Tho)/2.);
        Cc=Cp((Tci+Tco)/2.);
        }
    Qh=Fh*Ch*(Thi-Tho);
    Qc=Fc*Cc*(Tco-Tci);
    Qa=(Qc+Qh)/2.;
    U=Qa/area/LMTD(Thi-Tco,Tho-Tci);
    Umean+=U;
    Ui[i]=U;
    }

printf("sorting results\n");
qsort(Ui,cases,sizeof(double),CompareDoubles);

printf("filing results\n");
Umean/=cases;
Umin=Ui[0];
Umax=Ui[cases-1];
Umedian=(Umin+Umax)/2.;

fprintf(fp,"Umin=%lG\n",Umin);
fprintf(fp,"Umean=%lG\n",Umean);
fprintf(fp,"Umedian=%lG\n",Umedian);
fprintf(fp,"Umax=%lG\n",Umax);
```

```c
    i=(int)(cases*0.975);
    j=(int)(cases*0.025);
    U95=Ui[i]-Ui[j];
    fprintf(fp,"U95=%lG (%lG%%)\n",U95,100.*(U95/Umean));

    for(i=0;i<cases;i++)
       {
       j=(int)(((Ui[i]-Umin)*(bins-1))/(Umax-Umin));
       bin[j]++;
       }

    for(j=0;j<bins;j++)
       {
       U=Umin+(j+0.5)*(Umax-Umin)/bins;

       fprintf(fp,"%lf,%lf\n",U,0.121055*((double)bin[j])*((
       double)bins)/((double)cases));
       }

    free(bin);
    free(Ui);
    }

int main(int argc,char**argv,char**envp)
    {
    if((fp=fopen("UAbiased.csv","wt"))==NULL)
       {
       printf("can't create output file\n");
       return(1);
       }
    Calculate(0,0);
    Calculate(1,0);
    Calculate(1,1);
    fclose(fp);
    return(0);
    }
```

Appendix G. Diffusion Simulation Program

The following is a very simple Windows® program that draws a bunch of yellow dots on the screen and *rattles* them to simulate diffusion.

```
#include <stdlib.h>
#define _USE_MATH_DEFINES
#include <math.h>
#define WIN32_LEAN_AND_MEAN
#include <windows.h>

HINSTANCE hInst;
HWND hMain;
HWND hPush;
WORD ID=0x0100;
int busy;
int radius=40;

POINT*Particle;
int particles;

void ResetSimulation()
  {
  int p;
  RECT rc;
  GetClientRect(hMain,&rc);
  for(p=0;p<particles;p++)
    {
    do{
      Particle[p].x=rand()%(2*radius)-radius;
      Particle[p].y=rand()%(2*radius)-radius;
      }while(Particle[p].x*Particle[p].x+Particle[p].y
    *Particle[p].y>radius*radius);
    Particle[p].x+=rc.right/2;
    Particle[p].y+=rc.bottom/2;
    }
  }

int nint(double d)
  {
  if(d>0.)
    return((int)(d+0.5));
  if(d<0.)
    return((int)(d-0.5));
  return(0);
  }

LRESULT WINAPI MainProc(HWND hWnd,DWORD wMsg,DWORD
   wParam,LPARAM lParam)
  {
```

```
if(wMsg==WM_CLOSE)
  PostQuitMessage(0);

if(wMsg==WM_COMMAND)
  {
  if(HIWORD(wParam)==BN_CLICKED&&LOWORD(wParam)==ID)
    {
    if(busy)
      KillTimer(hMain,1);
    else
      {
      ResetSimulation();
      SetTimer(hMain,1,500,NULL);
      }
    busy=1-busy;
    SetWindowText((HWND)lParam,busy?"Stop":"Go");
    }
  return(FALSE);
  }

if(wMsg==WM_CREATE)
  return(FALSE);

if(wMsg==WM_PAINT)
  {
  int p;
  HDC hdc;
  PAINTSTRUCT pS;
  hdc=BeginPaint(hWnd,&pS);
  for(p=0;p<particles;p++)

  SetPixel(hdc,Particle[p].x,Particle[p].y,0x00FFFF);
  EndPaint(hWnd,&pS);
  return(FALSE);
  }

if(wMsg==WM_TIMER)
  {
  int a,p,r,u,v;
  RECT rc;
  GetClientRect(hMain,&rc);
  for(p=0;p<particles;p++)
    {
    r=1+rand()%20;
    a=rand()%360;
    u=nint(r*cos(M_PI*a/180.));
    v=nint(r*sin(M_PI*a/180.));
    Particle[p].x=max(0,min(rc.right-
1,Particle[p].x+u));
```

```c
      Particle[p].y=max(0,min(rc.bottom-
   1,Particle[p].y+v));
      }
    RedrawWindow(hMain,NULL,NULL,RDW_INVALIDATE|
    RDW_ERASE);
    return(FALSE);
    }

  return(DefWindowProc(hWnd,wMsg,wParam,lParam));
  }

int WINAPI WinMain(HINSTANCE hCurrent,HINSTANCE
   hPrevious,char*lCommand,int nShow)
  {
  int high,wide;
  MSG msg;
  WNDCLASS wc;

  hInst=hCurrent;

  memset(&wc,0,sizeof(WNDCLASS));
  wc.hInstance    =hInst;
  wc.hIcon        =LoadIcon(NULL,IDI_APPLICATION);
  wc.style        =CS_HREDRAW|CS_VREDRAW;
  wc.lpszClassName="MAIN";
  wc.lpfnWndProc  =(WNDPROC)MainProc;
  wc.hbrBackground=GetStockObject(BLACK_BRUSH);
  wc.hCursor      =LoadCursor(NULL,IDC_CROSS);
  RegisterClass(&wc);

  wide=GetSystemMetrics(SM_CXSCREEN);
  high=GetSystemMetrics(SM_CYSCREEN);

  hMain=CreateWindowEx(WS_EX_DLGMODALFRAME,"MAIN",
    "Diffusion Simulation",WS_POPUP|WS_CAPTION|
    WS_SYSMENU|WS_VISIBLE,wide/16,high/32,7*wide/8,
    7*high/8,NULL,NULL,hInst,NULL);
  hPush=CreateWindow("BUTTON","Go",WS_CHILD|
    WS_VISIBLE|BS_PUSHBUTTON,0,0,52,26,hMain,(void*)ID,
    hInst,NULL);

  particles=8192;
  Particle=calloc(particles,sizeof(POINT));
  ResetSimulation();
  RedrawWindow(hMain,NULL,NULL,RDW_INVALIDATE|
    RDW_ERASE);

  while(GetMessage(&msg,NULL,0,0))
    if(!TranslateMessage(&msg))
```

```
    DispatchMessage(&msg);

return((int)msg.wParam);
}
```

Appendix H. Password Synonym Finder

As presented in Chapter 13, Microsoft Office® uses the (rather pathetic) MD5 hash to encrypt passwords. This is easily cracked, as there are a very limited number of combinations and as many as 66 synonyms for each password. The following program and all of the inputs plus two batch files (one to compile and the other to launch) are included in the on-line archive in the "passwords" folder.

This program reads 191,215 words from a dictionary, 4907 proper names, 20,899 cities, 291 countries, 3999 Roman numerals, and 14,976 dates for a total of 236,287 potential passwords. After reading them all in, it sorts them and removes the 5001 duplicates. Then it indexes and hashes them before finding 3,061,094 synonyms. Finally, it lists a few examples. This entire process takes a whopping 1.032 seconds! Take that, Microsoft®! Like I said, Excel® is slower than a herd of snails stampeding up the side of a salt dome. You really need to learn C. Here's the program output:

```
synonyms words.txt names.txt cities.txt countries.txt
    roman.txt dates.txt
finding MD5 synonyms
words.txt: 191215 words, 45 longest, 0.297 seconds
names.txt: 4907 words, 13 longest, 0.000 seconds
cities.txt: 20899 words, 37 longest, 0.047 seconds
countries.txt: 291 words, 24 longest, 0.000 seconds
roman.txt: 3999 words, 15 longest, 0.016 seconds
dates.txt: 14976 words, 10 longest, 0.031 seconds
sorting 236287 words... 0.234 seconds
indexing... 5001 duplicates 0.016 seconds
hashing 231286 words... 0.000 seconds
finding synonyms... 3061094 (66) 0.391 seconds
total elapsed time... 1.032 seconds
3 random samples
Kaposvar
  sunbeams
  Westover
  sunrises
  Kaposvar
  Sunriver
  ingenues
  elamites
  initials
  Torretto Italy
Oconnor
  Gedicks
  sequels
  cumshaw
  engrams
  welkins
```

```
  Oconnor
  unstrap
  approachability
  Sorrels
  softens
  Alister
  infixer
Nesbyen-Skoglund
  professionalizer
  professionalized
  Nesbyen-Skoglund
```

Here's the source code:

```c
#define _CRT_SECURE_NO_DEPRECATE
#include <stdio.h>
#include <stdlib.h>
#include <string.h>
#include <malloc.h>
#define WIN32_LEAN_AND_MEAN
#include <windows.h>

size_t lrand()
  {
  size_t l1,l2,l3,l4;
  l1=(size_t)rand();
  l2=(size_t)rand();
  l3=(size_t)rand();
  l4=(size_t)rand();
  return(l1|(l2<<4)|(l3<<8)|(l4<<8));
  }

WORD MD5hash(BYTE*str,WORD len)
  {
  WORD l,w,v;
  for(w=l=0;l<len;l++)
    {
    v=str[l];
    v<<=l+1;
    w^=v;
    }
  w^=len;
  w^=0xCE4B;
  return(w);
  }

#define LONGEST 64

typedef struct{char txt[LONGEST+1];WORD hash;size_t
    l1,l2;}WRD;
```

```
WRD*Wrd;
size_t nwrd=0;
size_t mwrd=10000;

int CompareWord(const void*v1,const void*v2)
   {
   return(strcmp(((WRD*)v1)->txt,((WRD*)v2)->txt));
   }

int CompareHash(const void*v1,const void*v2)
   {
   WORD h1,h2;
   size_t j1,j2;
   j1=*((size_t*)v1);
   j2=*((size_t*)v2);
   h1=Wrd[j1].hash;
   h2=Wrd[j2].hash;
   if(h1<h2)
      return(-1);
   if(h1>h2)
      return(1);
   return(0);
   }

size_t*Idx;
size_t*Jdx;

int main(int argc,char**argv,char**envp)
   {
   char bufr[LONGEST+2],*ptr;
   size_t i,j,k,l,m,n,p,q,r,s;
   DWORD t0,t1,t2;
   FILE*fp;
   WRD*old;

   t0=t1=GetTickCount();
   printf("finding MD5 synonyms\n");
   if((Wrd=calloc(mwrd,sizeof(WRD)))==NULL)
      {
      printf("can't allocate memory\n");
      return(1);
      }

   for(i=1;i<(size_t)argc;i++)
      {
      printf("%s: ",argv[i]);
      fp=fopen(argv[i],"rt");
      m=n=0;
      while(fgets(bufr,sizeof(bufr),fp))
```

```
    {
    n++;
    l=strlen(bufr)-1;
    if(l<1)
      continue;
    if(l>m)
      m=l;
    ptr=strchr(bufr,'\n');
    if(ptr==NULL)
      {
      printf("\nword on line %u is too long (>%u
  characters)\n%s\n",n,(unsigned)LONGEST,bufr);
      return(1);
      }
    *ptr=0;
    if(nwrd>=mwrd)
      {
      old=Wrd;
      mwrd+=10000;
      if((Wrd=calloc(mwrd,sizeof(WRD)))==NULL)
        {
        printf("can't allocate memory\n");
        return(1);
        }
      memcpy(Wrd,old,nwrd*sizeof(WRD));
      free(old);
      }
    strcpy(Wrd[nwrd++].txt,bufr);
    }
  fclose(fp);
  t2=GetTickCount();
  printf("%u words, %u longest, %.3lf
  seconds\n",n,m,(t2-t1)/1000.);
  t1=t2;
  }

printf("sorting %u words... ",nwrd);
qsort(Wrd,nwrd,sizeof(WRD),CompareWord);
t2=GetTickCount();
printf("%.3lf seconds\n",(t2-t1)/1000.);
t1=t2;

printf("indexing... ");
if((Idx=calloc(nwrd,sizeof(size_t)))==NULL)
  {
  printf("\ncan't allocate memory\n");
  return(1);
  }
```

```
      for(m=l=1;l<nwrd;l++)
        if(strcmp(Wrd[l].txt,Wrd[l-1].txt))
          Idx[m++]=l;
      l-=m;
      if(l)
        printf("%u duplicate%s ",l,l!=1?"s":"");
      t2=GetTickCount();
      printf("%.3lf seconds\n",(t2-t1)/1000.);
      t1=t2;

      nwrd-=l;
      printf("hashing %u words... ",nwrd);
      if((Jdx=calloc(nwrd,sizeof(size_t)))==NULL)
        {
        printf("\ncan't allocate memory\n");
        return(1);
        }
      for(n=0;n<nwrd;n++)
        {
        i=Idx[n];
        Jdx[n]=i;
        Wrd[i].hash=MD5hash(Wrd[i].txt,strlen(Wrd[i].txt));
        }
      t2=GetTickCount();
      printf("%.3lf seconds\n",(t2-t1)/1000.);
      t1=t2;

      printf("finding synonyms... ");
      qsort(Jdx,nwrd,sizeof(size_t),CompareHash);

      for(s=n=m=k=0;k<nwrd;k++)
        {
        i=Idx[k];
        p=0;
        q=nwrd;
        for(r=0;r<32;r++)
          {
          l=(p+q)/2;
          j=Jdx[l];
          if(Wrd[j].hash<Wrd[i].hash)
            p=l;
          else if(Wrd[j].hash>Wrd[i].hash)
            q=l;
          else
            break;
          if(p==q)
            break;
          }
        while(l>0)
```

```
      {
      j=Jdx[l-1];
      if(Wrd[j].hash<Wrd[i].hash)
        break;
      l--;
      }
    Wrd[i].l1=Wrd[i].l2=l;
    for(;l<nwrd;l++)
      {
      j=Jdx[l];
      if(Wrd[j].hash>Wrd[i].hash)
        break;
      Wrd[i].l2=l;
      }
    n=Wrd[i].l2-Wrd[i].l1;
    if(n>m)
      m=n;
    s+=n;
    }
  printf("%u (%u) ",s,m);

  t2=GetTickCount();
  printf("%.3lf seconds\n",(t2-t1)/1000.);
  t1=t2;

  t2=GetTickCount();
  printf("total elapsed time... %.3lf seconds\n",(t2-
    t0)/1000.);

  n=3;
  printf("%u random samples\n",n);
  for(m=0;m<n;m++)
    {
    k=lrand()%nwrd;
    i=Idx[k];
    printf("%s\n",Wrd[i].txt);
    for(l=Wrd[i].l1;l<Wrd[i].l2;l++)
      printf("   %s\n",Wrd[Jdx[l]].txt);
    }

  return(0);
  }
```

also by D. James Benton

3D Rendering in Windows: How to display three-dimensional objects in Windows with and without OpenGL, ISBN-9781520339610, Amazon, 2016.

Curve-Fitting: The Science and Art of Approximation, ISBN-9781520339542, Amazon, 2016.

Evaporative Cooling: The Science of Beating the Heat, ISBN-9781520913346, Amazon, 2017.

Heat Exchangers: Performance Prediction & Evaluation, ISBN-9781973589327, Amazon, 2017.

Jamie2 2nd Ed.: Innocence is easily lost and cannot be restored, ISBN-9781520339375, Amazon, 2016-18.

Little Star 2nd Ed.: God doesn't do things the way we expect Him to. He's better than that! ISBN-9781520338903, Amazon, 2015-17.

Living Math: Seeing mathematics in every day life (and appreciating it more too), ISBN-9781520336992, Amazon, 2016.

Lost Cause: If only history could be changed…, ISBN-9781521173770. Amazon 2017.

Mill Town Destiny: The Hand of Providence brought them together to rescue the mill, the town, and each other, ISBN-9781520864679, Amazon, 2017.

ROFL: Rolling on the Floor Laughing, ISBN-9781973300007, Amazon, 2017.

A Synergy of Short Stories: The whole may be greater than the sum of the parts, ISBN-9781520340319, Amazon, 2016.

Thermodynamics - Theory & Practice: The science of energy and power, ISBN-9781520339795, Amazon, 2016.

Version-Independent Programming: Code Development Guidelines for the Windows® Operating System, ISBN-9781520339146, Amazon, 2016.

Printed in Great Britain
by Amazon